"Oh, may the Spirit of God place these life-changing truths deep in your heart. The words hidden in these pages will lift your walk in Christ to new levels of joy and peace! Fresh truths from the Word of God appear on every page."

Glenna Salsbury, speaker; author, *The Art of the Fresh Start*

"At the core of our being we long for a relationship with God that transforms surface faith into an intimate love relationship. With personal transparency, poignant biblical truth, and road-tested application, Debbie Alsdorf has given us the tools we need to go deeper with God. The reflections at the end of each chapter make this book an ideal resource for personal study and for small group interaction. I highly recommend it!"

Carol Kent, speaker; author, *A New Kind of Normal*

"Women need the truth. Lots of us believe we don't measure up and we must perform in order to be accepted. In *Deeper*, Debbie Alsdorf takes the reader on an honest and life-changing journey through four core truths found in Psalm 139. When a woman embraces these truths, she is set free! *Deeper* helps women understand God's love and involvement in every detail of life. Debbie embraced this depth of love and now beautifully teaches truth that changes a woman forever."

Jennifer Rothschild, author, *Lessons I Learned in the Dark* and *Self Talk, Soul Talk.*

"Are you sick of the shallow, rat-race, 'Stepford-like' Christian life? Long to go deeper with God and discover 'real' relationship with Christ? Debbie Alsdorf leads us to a deeper, richer, fuller love relationship with God. Every woman would love life more if she too went *Deeper*. Now every woman can because Debbie has blazed the trail to the deeper walk with God."

Pam Farrel, author, *Men Are Like Waffles,*
Women Are Like Spaghetti,

"In *Deeper*, Debbie Alsdorf shares practical, learned wisdom with all of us. As Debbie's pastor, co-worker, and friend I have observed her living out her faith every day for the last ten years. Debbie has helped so many people to reevaluate their actual worth based on what God has said and done, and not based upon anything hurtful (or flattering) that others would say or do. This healthy way of thinking requires following daily Scripture-based disciplines that, over time, transform our conscious and subconscious thought processes. In *Deeper*, Debbie shares essential core truths that have lifted her out of the mire of hurtful memories. I know firsthand that Debbie practices everything that she shares in *Deeper*. God's love for us is real, and it is deeper than any human love."

Steve Madsen, senior pastor, Cornerstone Fellowship

DEEPER

Living in the Reality of God's Love

Debbie Alsdorf

Revell

a division of Baker Publishing Group
Grand Rapids, Michigan

Published by Revell
a division of Baker Publishing Group
P.O. Box 6287, Grand Rapids, MI 49516-6287
www.revellbooks.com

Second printing, March 2008

Printed in the United States of America

Library of Congress Cataloging-in-Publication Data
Alsdorf, Debbie.
    Deeper : living in the reality of God's love / Debbie Alsdorf.
       p.   cm.
    Includes bibliographical references.
    ISBN 978-0-8007-3215-8 (pbk.)
       1. Christian women—Religious life. 2. Spirituality. 3. God. I. Title.
    BV4527.A455 2008
    248.8′43—dc22   2007040846

To Jinny, Mary Lou, and Becky. I will always be grateful for how you lived the truth of God's love and grace in front of me so many years ago. You taught me more than you can imagine. And to Lorri, my technicolor friend who lives deeply as God's daughter. You inspire me to continue walking in the reality of God's love.

Contents

Everything got started in him and finds its purpose in him.

Colossians 1:16 Message

Acknowledgments

Many thanks to:

My family—Ray, Justin, Ashley, Megan, and Cameron. I am a very blessed wife, mother, and stepmother! I love you so much. Each of you is a gift.

My sister Sharon—there is nobody like you in my life. Love you forever!

Les Stobbe—you are more than an agent, you are an answer to prayer.

Vicki Crumpton—thanks for editing with heart and patience. I could not have asked for a better experience or a better editor.

All the women who have told me their stories, opened their hearts, and allowed me to be part of their healing. You know who you are. I know your stories will now touch other women.

The Design4Living prayer team, led by Voni Ribera—you prayed for this message to be in print and for God to open doors. He did! Thanks, Voni!

The women at Cornerstone Fellowship—I love serving you and being part of your lives. Let's keep growing deeper.

Ali Contois—thank you for prayers, support, and tomatoes! God is moving in your life with his love. It's exciting to be part of it.

Terry Perazza—thanks for all the miles logged and time spent traveling with me, sitting in airports, setting up book tables, and all that fun stuff. You have heard this message over and over, and the way God has touched your life continues to inspire me.

Eileen Terpstra—I love how you challenge me to love Jesus, trust Jesus, and walk in the Spirit.

My dear friend Lorri Steer. Being part of your life and having you call me "mentor" has humbled me and changed me forever. I stand in awe at how God is moving in your life.

The women's staff team at Cornerstone Fellowship—you are amazing! Your hard work has enabled me to continue to stretch, grow, and develop as a woman in ministry and leadership. Thank you BethAnn, Susan Z., Susan T., and Sheree, the Core Team, BLTs, the Wild Teams, Kristina, Terry, and all the many volunteers.

The Fab Four—you know who you are! I love you girls. Love you, love you, love you! Your friendships are irreplaceable.

Sue Boldt—I know Jesus because of you! Need I say more?

BethAnn Moitoso—Beth, Beth, Beth, what a gift you have been! That says it all.

My heavenly Father—you have restored my life, have set a new song in my heart, a new spring in my step, and have given me a new hope for tomorrow.

Introduction

The Beginning of Something Deeper

You know there has to be more; you're just not sure how to get there. One thing is certain; you just don't want to stay where you are at.

Charles Swindoll

My Christian experience has been like two completely different books. The first volume I call *Christianity Lite*, an instruction manual to a Stepford Woman reality. I knew how to say and do the right things, filled myself up with lots of biblical knowledge, and served in the local church—but I had very little real-life transformation. Even though I looked the part and played the part, my life was filled with secret shame and hidden hang-ups. My theology did not match my reality, and so my life was more about me than about Christ.

Then came volume 2.

The Stepford Woman crashed and burned. My life as I knew it fell apart. As circumstances went from bad to worse, my life seemed out of control and insanely empty. I was suddenly living a life I'd never dreamed existed. I needed something more than being part of a big Christian club, something more than looking good and doing good. I needed real hope in a real God.

Hoping for something different took courage.

My life at that point had been full of messy pieces and loose ends. I had stuffed them, suppressed them, and tried to cover over them. But somewhere along the way I quit hiding and began to be real about my brokenness. And after spending most of my life wondering who I was and if my life mattered, I began to learn the truth about my existence and the love of the God who created me. I began to seek after the God who promised abundant life, and I desperately wanted to know what that life really was. I dared to hope that it wasn't just a Christian cliché that I had learned to recite over the years. I hoped it was reality and that abundance of life was meant for people like me.

Because I arrived at the place of wanting something different in my spiritual life, I realized I had to quit doing the same ol' things I had always done. I needed to stop the insanity and try something new. So I made a decision to start over in my walk with God, and after seventeen years of being a believer I made the choice to get more serious about my faith.

Slowly my theology began to match reality. I began to see God for who he is, and see myself as someone belonging to him. I began to have a faith in God that was authentic and practical— the kind of faith that helped me live differently in the ordinary places of life.

I want this kind of living to become the foundation for us as women today—women who face the pressure to perform and to conform to our culture in order for our worth to be recognized. Women who live in a world that applauds "doing something" and cares very little about "being someone." When we know the reality of God's love and faithfulness and learn to live in the truth of that love daily, we will discover something deeper—his pulse in the ordinary places of our everyday lives. This spiritual reality is the beginning of a different way of living—a calling back to truth.

Oswald Chambers wrote that "once you are rooted in reality, nothing can shake you."[1] Let's get rooted, real, and unshakable— and learn to live like all that Christ is and who we are in him is real.

Excited to be sharing this journey with you,
Debbie Alsdorf

/

Dancing with Angels

A Mother's Last Words to Her Daughter

> Once we truly see God at work, we will never be concerned again about the things that happen, because we are actually trusting in our Father in heaven, whom the world cannot see.
>
> Oswald Chambers

Life happens. Circumstances rub us the wrong way, and often our Christian experience is not the life-changing reality it was meant to be. Instead of an authentic encounter with God, our relationship with him is often reduced to a brave face, good works, and a bandage for the bumps in life. We usually don't admit our restlessness or our emptiness; instead we just try harder to get it right, going through the motions of pulling ourselves together. We wrestle in the deepest parts of us and wonder if there's something more. We may have given up on wishing upon a star and grown beyond fairy-tale thinking, but at the deepest level we still wish for the sparkle, that something special that's real enough to fill the void within our hearts, to take the drab out of our daily life—and to change us.

God Has a Way of Making Himself Real to Us

It was a sad and difficult summer. My sister and I with the assistance of hospice were taking care of our mother during her final days. Though the sun was bright outside, all was dark inside as we watched our once fiery mother grow weaker by the day. Always a strong woman, she fought her pending death even though her body was giving up. At the urging of the hospice nurse, I once again talked with my mom about letting go.

"It's okay to let go," I whispered as I took her frail hand in mine. "We know you are going to be with Jesus, so really, Mom, it's okay."

"No! I'm *not* going anywhere without you and the boys," she snapped with defiance.

"Mom, I think you'll have to. It's your time and not ours."

Her lower lip began quivering. "Well, that's easy for you to say! You are there and I am here. We better hope everything we've believed in is real!"

Shocked, I realized that my mom was afraid—very afraid—to die.

I had never thought much about it before, but in my naïveté it hadn't occurred to me that Christians might actually be afraid to die. After all, we talk about the promises of God and say we believe in eternal life. We even sing songs about his amazing grace and heaven. But, now nearing the fulfillment of his promises to her, my mom—definitely a Christian—was scared to death.

Her fear broke my heart. I began praying that God would make himself real to her and free her from the anxiety that was written all over her face. That was Monday.

God Has a Way of Touching Us

Friday morning I woke to a call telling me to get over to my sister's house. My mom was in the "rally" stage. We had been prepared for this, that near the end some patients exhibit a final burst of energy. But though hospice educated and prepared us for the stages of death, nothing could have prepared me for that day.

Sitting up in bed for the first time all week, my mom was beaming with joy and happiness. This wasn't the fear-struck woman of Monday morning. No, now she had a smile larger than any I had ever seen, and a radiance that seemed to light up the room.

"Debbie! It's so fancy there!" she told me with childlike excitement as I made my way to her bedside. My mother never used words like *fancy*, so that took me by surprise and got my attention.

"Where?" I asked, my heart nearly beating out of my chest.

"Sit down and I'll tell you all about it," she said as she straightened herself up.

I sat down next to her bed, and she began to tell me about her glimpses of heaven. She spoke of angels, emeralds as big as boulders, and streets shining like glass. She was especially intrigued that there seemed to be "appointment times" for each of us to get in.

She was ready and excited to go and wanted me to know that everything we believed in was real—so real that she had no desire to stay on earth any longer.

I looked over to see her nurse, who had tears streaming down her face, quietly mouthing to me, "It's real. She's not on any meds ... this is real!" This clearly wasn't drug-induced hysteria or hallucination. My mom, though dying, was not medicated. She was coherent, sharp, and determined to tell me about the reality of heaven and what she was seeing. The next hour was filled with her laying it all out for me—piece by piece. I had never seen my mother like this; I knew it was real.

In her excitement, she asked me to go get my two sons so she could tell them. I rushed across town and back with lightning speed. We visited a little and then sang a few of her favorite church songs. As we sang she looked around the room in wonder, smiling and nodding to things we couldn't see. When we finished singing she smiled and told the boys, "Oh, you sound so much more beautiful with the angels." My oldest son, a typical seventeen-year-old, corrected her, "No, Grandma, it's just us." "Oh no, it's not, this room is filled with angels." She smiled confidently at her vision of the heavenly realm dancing over us.

Now was the time for good-byes. She motioned my oldest son, Justin, over to her side. She cleared her throat and began, "Justin, you have always been Grandma's big blond boy. I have never wanted to leave you. But, you know those angels that it talks about in the Bible? Well, you know how they are supposed to keep us in all our ways? Well, I always wondered about that, but now I know it's true. They're real. I've seen them, so I don't have to worry anymore. You're safe. Just promise Grandma one last thing before I go . . ."

20

Sobbing, my son managed to muffle out, "Anything, Grandma, anything."

"Justin, live like it's real, because it is!" Crying, he hugged her, then found a corner of the room to nestle in and console himself while his younger brother, Cameron, made his way to Grandma's bedside. Even though he was thirteen, Cameron became like a little boy all over again, hanging on to his grandma's every word. Sniffling up tears, Cameron nodded to her quiet request, as once again she said, "Will you promise Grandma one thing?" With the same gut-wrenching sobs his brother had, he too managed to squeak out, "Yes, Grandma." As she gave him a final hug she repeated the same message, "Live like it's real, because it is."

Now it was my turn. I figured we would get emotional and declare our love for each other . . . you know, maybe something like, "My darling daughter, how I have loved you . . ." But there was no emotionalism in her last words to me. Instead she was getting very tired, almost to the point of running out of energy. She motioned me close to her and pulled on my collar, bringing my face right up to hers. Her faded brown eyes now looked stern and serious as she began to speak to me.

"Debra."

Uh-oh, she only called me Debra if I was in trouble or if she was very serious. This was not going to be an emotional scene; she had something important to say. Almost like a mother's last command, she gave me a firm charge: "Live like it's real, because it is." Crying and unable to speak, I nodded. Always a mother, she threw in one last word: "And those women you speak to—tell them to spend their lives living like it's real."

I was stunned that she repeated this message to us three times. There was no last "I love you," no final reminiscing, just the clear and uncut message of those four words: *live like it's real*. As I stood by the rented hospital bed, surrounded by crumpled Kleenex, I knew something profound had just taken place. In the middle of my ordinary life, I had just been in the center of a holy moment—one that I will never forget. It took my mom a lifetime, but now at the time of her death, she had found the sparkle, and it lit her up with faith, hope, and love in a fashion uncharacteristic of her normal self.

She slept most of the next few days. Occasionally she woke and spoke to other family members, repeating things like "It's so fancy there" and "I'm ready to go." My sister got one last "I love you," but I never heard my mother's voice again; those four words, on her final Friday, were the last words she ever spoke to me.

She died peacefully a few days later at her appointed time.

Life Is Waiting for Us

The meaning behind my mother's words is more about life than death. Sure, she wanted us to know that heaven is real, but the reason behind the knowing was so that God himself could capture our hearts now and forever change our perspective about the way we live.

It was amazing to see the transformation of a woman who was bound by fear to a woman who was completely released from that fear. What she saw changed her. I began to hope that I could be changed too.

Even though I had been a Christian for many years, the eight years leading up to my mom's death had been hard. I had gone through divorce, illness, remarriage, and relocation. After losing so much and ending up in the pit of clinical depression, I began the journey of getting real with God, going back to the basics of faith, while fighting to reclaim my life and stability. Those were tough years. Some days I didn't think I would make it. But God was faithful and through the pain began showing me the reality of his love for me. The children's song "Jesus Loves Me" began to take on a whole new meaning as the truth of those song lyrics began to travel from head to heart. Slowly I began to experience spiritual change in a way I had never known before.

I began sharing the reality of God's love with women of all ages. During those years my elderly mother moved in with us. She helped with the kids, and we helped with her medical care. Our wounded mother-daughter relationship began to heal, and life was moving along at a steady clip. And, just as I was starting over, learning how to lean into God's love, my mother's chronic health issues took a turn for the worse. Before I knew it she was gone.

God Has a Way of Changing Us

The day she died I felt empty. More empty than I'd ever felt before. My root system had been pulled from me. My father had died years earlier, so now with both parents gone I was officially an orphan. And though I was in my early forties I felt like I was five years old. I cried like a baby and tried to find hope in the words she left me.

As the grieving process went on, I was daily reminded of her words. I could hear her say, "Debra, live like it's real, because it is." I could see her aged brown eyes staring through me as she spoke them. Slowly I began to realize that her words were a gift from God. They were words about faith in the Almighty, faith in the truth of Scripture, faith in the relevance of finally making Christ my life—my total life.

It's been several years since her death, and those words still echo through me. I have come to understand that I am not an orphan, not alone, and not left to fend for myself. I belong to the Almighty. I have been growing steadily as his woman—baby step by baby step. I am watching as old fears and insecurities are steadily diminishing bit by bit. And, yes, I have kept my promise—I close every speaking engagement with those last words, "Live like it's real, because it is!"

Now I write this book praying that you will find something within these pages to reenergize your faith in God, sharpen your focus, and define you in a way that makes everything different. Though my mother's words were about her glimpses of heaven as she was facing death, the words in this book are about living toward heaven in this life. To have this new perspective, we must know the power and promise of God's love as our new reality. We must also believe the truth of who we are and, more importantly, whose we are. When responding to this love we will discover a life of surrender and living beyond just ourselves.

We were created to live in his purpose for us, rest in his love for us, and move through life depending on his power within us. But many of us are so locked up in ourselves that we don't experience his purpose. Jesus said that truth will set us free.

There is one particular truth that will set you free to experience what you were created for. You see, the truest thing about you is the truth that you are his. This truth declares that you are his treasure and that you are in good, powerful, and loving hands. You belong to the Most High God. This is what is real. The picture is bigger than we have ever imagined and more real than we ever hoped it could be.

Will you dare to hug this truth close to your heart?

Will you dare to learn how to live like it's real?

As truth is embraced, I can promise you this—you will find yourself being set free. And this promise of freedom isn't coming from me, it's much more solid than that. This promise comes straight from God, who sent his Son, Jesus, for the purpose of restoring and rebuilding our lives. This is the good news—life happens and Jesus shows up to set us free from the reality of the pain, confusion, and emptiness. I'm stepping into this new life and learning to live like the simple truth of God's love is real—will you join me?

We were meant to live for so much more than ourselves.

And he died for all, that those who live should no longer live for themselves but for him.

2 Corinthians 5:15

I can hear him calling me to a deeper place. It's a call for all who want something more.

He is calling . . .

Come to me and learn to live differently.

Come and discover a new reality.

Come to me and learn whose you are.

Come to me and learn to live like it's real.

For Further Reflection

1. What's your reality? Is it just what you can see today or does it extend into a bigger picture that would be defined as faith?
2. Do you live according to a faith-based reality or do your daily actions reflect just your feelings and your self?
3. What would it take to change your life?
4. Would living like it's real cause you to make adjustments and live differently?

Step 1

Getting Real with God

Moving Beyond Myself in Order to Find Myself in Him

If our love relationship with God is to grow, we must be ruthlessly honest with Him and let Him be ruthlessly honest with us. We must above all give Him time—time in which we can expose the real core of our being. We must dare to be real and open and vulnerable with Him.

Tim Hansel

Real

authentic, genuine, not fake, basic, essential, serious.

Getting real with God is taking a good, honest look at who you are, where your life is, and what your spiritual life consists of. It's taking off church masks, moving away from facades, and making a decision to do the hard work of coming clean before the Almighty.

Getting real is admitting you are not perfect and never will be. It is accepting that your life is not perfect and wasn't meant to be—embracing that only God is perfect. When a woman moves beyond self-imposed or culturally imposed un-realistic expectations, she changes. In this place she becomes authenti-cally his. There is something genu-ine about her faith walk, something serious about her choices, and something new, streamlined, and basic about her belief system. As she moves away from all facades, a new joy permeates her. This joy is infectious. This joy gives her pas-sion for life again.

This kind of authenticity cannot be done without an understanding of the nature of God's love. As the truth of God's love begins to sink in, things change. In honesty and humility a new kind of life can begin. But it all starts with the first step—getting real with God.

2

Believing I'm Not Enough
The Painful Trap of Old Messages

> Self-rejection is the greatest enemy of the spiritual life because it contradicts the sacred voice that calls us the "Beloved." Being the Beloved expresses the core truth of our existence.
>
> Henri Nouwen

Like most young women, I had wished that my prince would come, and he did. We married young and planned to spend our days together serving the Lord. We had built our life around two darling sons and the large church my husband started as a home Bible study. After thirteen years of marriage our life appeared to be a picket-fence reality of spiritual and personal success. All was well, or so I thought, until the day my husband came home and told me the words that no woman ever wants to hear: "Debbie, I have never loved you."

At first I thought I was hearing things. I asked my husband to repeat what he was trying to tell me. He tried to be gentle, but there was nothing that could have softened the blow of words that cut to the deepest part of me. My husband, my pastor, my very best friend, didn't love me—and apparently never had.

Those words began to unravel our lives. In short order he was forced to resign from the pastorate, and within months I was served divorce papers. The humiliation associated with a ministry divorce is beyond words. I felt like a complete failure.

My frame of reference was rocked. I went from being the pastor's wife, Bible study teacher, director of women's ministry, Awana leader, and second-grade room mom to being a single mother of two young boys, struggling to survive in every way—spiritually, emotionally, physically, and financially. It was like a bad dream that I just wanted to wake up from.

I began to face personal feelings of worthlessness head on. Over and over again those words—you are not loved, never have been loved—kept playing through my mind. I had always struggled with insecurities, but now the battle took me down for the count. If I wasn't worth loving then I was certain that my life must be of little value. I was certain that I was no longer useful, no longer wanted, and no longer safe in God's hands. My circumstances screamed, "You are not enough—never have been, never will be." I felt like I had the word *loser* tattooed on my forehead.

But my story doesn't start or end with one set of circumstances. The divorce added fuel to the secretly burning embers of shame, insecurity, and worthlessness—a fire that had started many years earlier.

Words Will Never Hurt Me?

I used to think that those words *not enough* were familiar only to me. I thought I was the only one who struggled with feelings of being "less than." I have come to find out that many women struggle with trying to measure up.

For years I had defined myself by what I did or didn't accomplish, by the opinion of others, or by the self-defeating lies that took residence in my mental space. My definition and perception of myself was my most vulnerable place. This same place of vulnerability negatively affects many women today, because we have learned to define ourselves by standards that are not easily reached. The wrong definition can affect everything. Why? Because what defines us will eventually drive us.

> **Define**: to outline clearly what something is, to make distinct and clear.

> **Drive**: to compel into action, to cause to move in a given direction.

What defines you? How do you identify yourself? What essential qualities stand out in your mind that make up "you"—both good and bad? Believe it or not, the definition you have of yourself will compel your actions and choices—ultimately moving you through life.

If that definition is negative, unhealthy, or untrue, then you have a real problem on your hands. If you are defined by what you do, then you will always be pleasing people, performing perfectly, and running in circles. Faulty definitions of ourselves cause us to act in ways that aren't true to who we really are. When steeped in insecurities, a woman often acts in ways she doesn't understand

and unconsciously begins to live a life that is affected by her negative thinking.

Henri Nouwen observed,

> Over the years, I have come to realize that the greatest trap in our life is not success, popularity, or power, but self-rejection. When we have come to believe in the voices that call us worthless and unlovable, then success, popularity, and power are easily perceived as attractive solutions. The real trap, however, is self-rejection. As soon as someone accuses me or criticizes me, as soon as I am rejected, left alone, or abandoned, I find myself thinking, "Well that proves once again that I am nobody." . . . [My dark side says] I am no good . . . I deserved to be pushed aside, forgotten, rejected, and abandoned. Self-rejection is the greatest enemy of the spiritual life because it contradicts the sacred voice that calls us the "Beloved." Being the Beloved constitutes the core truth of our existence.[1]

Defining Moments

When I was young my dad brought home a player piano. That piano became my first best friend. I sang with those old rolls of songs for hours. Music rapidly became part of me. Before long, my parents, thinking they had discovered some talent, enrolled me in private voice lessons in Los Angeles, where I spent years training to sing and perform. I was now on the fast track to gaining attention.

Performing began to define me. Daddy loved to come hear me sing. When I performed, my dad didn't spend so much time in bars, which made my mom a little calmer. So the one thing I could do to control my little world was perform. It worked for the moment, and I could pretend that life was good, that I was good.

During my childhood my mother and I were emotionally disconnected, and I can remember longing for her love. I learned that love was conditional and required following strict rules. I worked hard at following her expectations to a T. When I brought home the A's she required, she never said a word. But when I brought home anything less than, the words flew with fury. Without anyone verbalizing it, I learned from a young age that anything less than perfect was not acceptable.

I wanted to be rescued from my life, and like most little girls I longed to be magically transformed into a Disney princess. But instead of a fairy godmother coming to the rescue, I lived through years of trying to be good enough.

When I was a senior in high school, I was voted homecoming queen. Naturally I was very excited about this high-ranking teenage honor. After years of a rocky relationship with a critical mother who picked me apart at every turn, this victory assured me of the acceptance I longed for.

The morning after the homecoming dance I woke up to the smell of freshly brewed coffee. I jumped out of bed and took my sparkling little tiara to where my mother was reading the paper. I danced into the room, excited to share my joy with the woman whom I lived my life trying to please. "Look, Mom, I'm the queen!" I twirled and giggled until she looked up and stunned me by saying, "They must have miscounted the votes." Crushed, I knew then that I was not enough and would never be enough for my mother.

Fast forward . . . many years later. The day I was blindsided with those words "I have never loved you" once again confirmed my childhood definition of not being enough. I wasn't woman enough, obviously not pretty enough, not wife enough. Not enough. Never had been—never would be.

For most of us the message of not being enough starts as early as the kindergarten playground. It's there that we learn which girls are the prettiest, which girls get chased the most by the boys, and which girls the other girls like. Our concept of who we are and who we should be gets its start when we are very young. Without knowing it, we then spend years in the developing solution of the world we live in, the friends we hang out with, and the dynamics of the families we are part of.

We Are Who We Have Been Becoming

Our belief system starts forming in our earliest days and continues throughout life. We need our minds renewed daily so that we don't keep turning back to the old thought patterns, self-rejection, or the principles of the world we live in. The greatest thing that can happen to us is learning to lean into the truth of God's Word and learning to live in the freedom of being his children. But for some reason, we stay stuck. Turning back to our old ways of thought and reasoning has always been a problem. Listen to what the apostle Paul says in the New Testament book of Galatians:

> So also, when we were children, we were in slavery under the basic principles of the world.... Formerly, when you did not know God, you were slaves to those who by nature are not gods. But now that you know God—or rather are known by God—how is it that you are turning back to those weak and miserable principles? Do you wish to be enslaved by them all over again?
>
> Galatians 4:3, 8–9

And then Paul speaks some similar words in the book of Ephesians:

34

As for you, you were dead in your transgressions and sins, in which you used to live when you followed the ways of this world and of the ruler of the kingdom of the air. . . . All of us also lived among them at one time, gratifying the cravings of our sinful nature and following its desires and thoughts. . . . But because of his great love for us, God, who is rich in mercy, made us alive with Christ.

2:1–4

My family life gave me poor spiritual programming. I learned to believe in God as a crisis manager, not as a heavenly Father who loved me. He was more like a taskmaster in the sky. I attended church every Sunday with my mom, but God was not part of our regular life—not in thought, word, or deed. Church attendance was just a religious duty.

In contrast, my friend Amy was raised in a Christian home where she was taught from a young age how to have a relationship with God. She attended church from the time she was cradled in her mother's arms and practically cut her teeth on Bible verses. But her friends at school became her world, and over time she gave in to peer pressure, beginning a journey of learning to conform to the acceptable standard of the group she was in. This conforming caused her to constantly pick herself apart and led to years of an eating disorder. Those negative patterns didn't go away overnight. As she became an adult and later a mother, she was troubled by how self-conscious and insecure she was—even as a Christian. She desperately wanted to conquer her insecurities because she didn't want to pass them on to her daughter. Over time she realized that she had missed something very important along the way—she wasn't sure who she really was or if her life mattered. Yes, even Amy, who was raised in the church, singing "Jesus Loves Me," was affected by the trap that she would have to "do" something more or "measure up" to be someone of significance.

What We Believe Becomes Part of Us

All of us have been affected by earlier messages. During that time we were unconsciously developing habits of thought and habits of behavior. Most of us picked up beliefs that are opposite of the truth of God's heart toward us. These beliefs become part of us, and old patterns are sometimes hard to identify and even harder to break.

While I was growing up I was conditioned by my circumstances. I learned how to live in self-consciousness, shame, and rejection. The roots of rejection were so tangled around my heart that they became who I was at the core of me; being "not enough" was the secret shame that defined me. And, being defined as such, I tried to live in ways that would compensate for who I felt I was—pleasing others at all costs, performing, hiding who the real me was, denying my feelings, not recognizing my own needs, chronic insecurity, and fear of failure. Many other women have learned to hide and live in unhealthy places too, some without even realizing it.

The years we spent being programmed by the world we live in have affected each of us. Even being raised in church does not provide immunity from wrong thinking. We can go to church our entire lives, but if truth has not become our reality, chances are we will develop wrong thinking over the years too.

I used to wish that when I accepted Christ some switch would be flipped, or a delete button pushed, forever erasing all the faulty thinking that had been building in me over the years. But I have since accepted, as verified here in Scripture, that because I have spent years learning the wrong things, I now must spend time relearning what is true, as one who is alive in Christ. If I don't embrace the truth, I will be forever enslaved to the weak and miserable expectations and the principles, thoughts, and defined identities of this world—even as a believer.

Once I realized that I needed to bring my perceived identity and my habits of thinking and responding to Christ for healing, my life began to change dramatically. Unfortunately, I didn't realize my true need for this until after I had been a Christian for seventeen years and came to a breaking point. Old thoughts don't just disappear. Most of the negative things we have come to believe about ourselves are lies, and we will need to work intentionally to be freed of their impact. Jesus himself tells us in the book of John that Satan, our enemy, "was a murderer from the beginning, not holding to the truth, for there is no truth in him. When he lies, he speaks his native language, for he is a liar and the father of lies" (John 8:44).

The world's way is led by a liar who is masquerading as light. Without realizing it, we learn to march behind his band, not even aware that we are keeping beat to the wrong drummer. It's time to get real about our negative perceptions and unscriptural definitions—both keep us locked up in defeat.

> Do not conform any longer to the pattern of this world, but be transformed by the renewing of your mind.
>
> Romans 12:2

> Don't become so well adjusted to your culture that you fit into it without even thinking. Instead fix your attention on God. You'll be changed from the inside out.
>
> Romans 12:2 Message

Pretty, Perfect, and Polished

We live in a culture that defines a woman in terms of appearance, accomplishments, and possessions. It's all about being pretty, perfect, and polished. And even if we poke fun at that thought, on some level we do work hard to become all three. If it's not our physical looks, it's our homes, our careers, or our bank account. Later it's often our children that we try to fit into the picture-perfect mold. And if we can't produce, it just proves the "not enough" idea once again.

A newspaper article focused on the pressure young women are facing today. "A typical American teenage girl will process over 3,000 advertisements in a single day and 10 million by the time they reach 18." The article goes on to quote a media critic, "You know, advertising has always sold anxiety and it certainly sells anxiety to the young. It's always telling them that they are not thin enough, they're not pretty enough, they don't have the right friends, or they have no friends. They're losers unless they're cool."[2] It's a sad statement for our young women today: acceptance is in the eye of the beholder—the media—and the media is selling anxiety by constantly trying to convince us to measure up in some way.

If today's teen processes 3,000 advertisements a day, just think how many that will be in her lifetime. And as for us grown women, don't be fooled; we've processed way too many ourselves. And each and every image had its own effect on us—whether we realized it or not.

The emphasis on being pretty, perfect, and polished has crept into our thinking, into our churches, and into our expectations of ourselves. There seems to be some invisible measuring stick that we are measuring ourselves with—or beating ourselves and others up with!

Meet Betty

Christian women experience a double whammy that makes the pressure to be perfect much harder to bear than what their unbelieving friends experience. Why? Because we try to measure up to two separate standards. On one side we have Betty Beautiful, our culture's standard, and on the other side we have Betty Believer, the unspoken standard in the church.

Betty Beautiful is the perfect woman. Otherwise known as a "ten." She is beautiful, successful, and educated. She is a mix of Betty Crocker, Mother Teresa, Wonder Woman, and a supermodel. And unlike the Betty Crocker of the past, this one is the updated version with a BMW, designer fashions, a loving family, and fame and fortune. She never has a bad hair day, never has a bad home day, never gains a pound, has her own personal trainer, and always looks like she's off the cover of a magazine. Betty Beautiful is forever sexy, slim, and stunning—she has it all. And Betty Beautiful never grows old—no hot flashes, no whiskers, no thinning hair, no mental-pause.

As Christians we are affected by her image. She is all around us—on the billboards, in the movies, in the magazines, and in the ads. Though we don't admit it, we are affected by the pressure to be her. Though we all know it's just a media image and that we will never measure up, we still unconsciously try. But Christian women don't stop at Betty Beautiful; they add Betty Believer into the mix.

Betty Believer's resume is impressive. She is everything that Betty Beautiful is—and then some. Betty Believer is the perfect ten and the perfect Proverbs 31 woman all rolled into one. Betty Believer leaps tall trials with a single bound, never has a bad hair day, a bad home day, or a worn-out faith day. She serves in the church, in the community, in the mission field, and takes meals to those in need. She always says the right thing at the right time, smiles even when she doesn't want to, and is liked by everyone who knows her. Her children are well behaved, never rebel, and are always gushing over her. She is the dictionary definition of *sweet*.

Don't forget that she rises while it's still dark to read her Bible, pray for her family, and tend her garden—the perfect balance of Mary and Martha. She never has a hot flash, an extra pound, or a wrinkled outfit. Though she is whirling with activity, she never misses the opportunity to bless someone or shoot up a prayer to heaven. And, as if all this isn't enough, she even manages to keep the family's magic moments and memories preserved in beautiful scrapbooks, doing Creative Memories in her spare time!

Now, seriously, do you really think we can ever measure up to standards so high? I don't think so. We laugh at the thought, but deep within us are those two nagging words—*not enough*. And somehow in a culture that drives home the message that we must be pretty, perfect, and polished, we end up knowing that we are *not enough*—never were, never will be. Then add to our dysfunction the idea that we have to be "spiritual enough" and we might as well jump off the next cliff we see.

Unfortunately the three P's don't begin and end with our appearance or abilities—they even extend to the way we view our lives. We begin to think that if our lives are not polished and in pretty packaging, then we aren't enough. With this mentality there is no room for messy pieces, stray ends, or imperfect business. It's easy to see how we can get trapped into thinking nothing is ever enough—not the right house, the right neighborhood, the right car. Some women even begin thinking that they don't have the right husband or family. What a trap!

Position, Passion, and Purpose

In God's economy there are three other P's that are much more important than being pretty, perfect, and polished, and they are position, passion, and purpose. The Bible makes it clear that people do look at our appearance, but even clearer is that God looks at our hearts. The heart is the core of us, the part of us that no one can see. And it is at this center place that we need to know:

> **Position**: Who am I? What is the truth about me? What defines me?

> **Passion**: What compels me, moves me, or drives me?

> **Purpose**: What am I living for? Why do I exist?

The messages of our past are powerful, but they do not have to rule our lives today. Most of the things we have believed about ourselves do not line up with God's truth about us. We have embraced the lies of a culture, the lies of the enemy, or the opinions of people—all are easy and natural to do. But God has a better way. He desires truth in the inward parts of us. It is truth that will set us free. We don't understand how it works, but it does.

As I walked through the valley of rejection and divorce, I had to come face-to-face with the reality that I had spent my life performing. I was so wrapped up in trying to make up for my deeply hidden insecurities that I was trapped in trying to attain the pretty, perfect, and polished image. Obviously that didn't work.

I came to a place where I had the need to get real and take the other three P's seriously. I realized that the deeper things had never been my emphasis. My attention always gravitated to the surface things—appearances and what others thought of me. After many years as a believer, I still didn't have a clue about my position in Christ. I knew a lot of the "to do" verses, but I didn't know how to live in the truth of Christ's unconditional grace and love for me. But in my new broken state, all of this nonsense was finally coming to an end. God himself was reaching down to stop the insanity.

Are You Trapped?

When we get stuck in our old messages, we become trapped. According to good ol' Webster's, a trap is a device to capture and kill something. In the same way, Satan, the enemy of our souls, the father of lies, the hissing serpent, has always wanted to keep us trapped. If he could just keep us bound up, we would be too immobilized or too self-focused to even consider living for God; we would never get real about our true identity but instead stay stuck in the facade of who we think we should be. Abundance? We would never experience it.

I used to think that abundant life was a Christian cliché, a pat answer given to church people to keep them hoping and to lift their spirits. A little like bread crumbs thrown to us for the journey. As Christians we find it easy to wonder where abundant life is, or if it is just for a select spiritual few. This is right where Satan wants us—believing in some of the truth but not fully convinced that Christ himself is the truth. Truth is a person that came and died to set us free. Satan, the father of lies, viciously opposes this type of truth-finding relationship with the living God. If he can keep us stuck in just enough faith to get us by, he will be happy. But God's plan is for us to have an experience of faith that becomes the air we breathe and the very lifeblood of who we are.

Jesus speaks of this in the Gospel of John:

> The thief comes only to steal and kill and destroy; I have come that they may have life, and have it to the full.
>
> John 10:10

Then you will know the truth, and the truth will set you free.

John 8:32

I am the way and the truth and the life.

John 14:6

Turning Our Lives Around

This "not enough" issue is addressed in the Bible by the apostle Paul. If anyone had room to boast, feel accomplished, or think they were pretty great, it would have been him. He was educated, accomplished, and admired by the people of his time. For women, that's the equivalent of being pretty, perfect, and polished! But even he, and the Christians in those days, must have struggled with wrong messages, because look at what he says:

> Such confidence as this is ours through Christ before God. Not that we are competent in ourselves to claim anything for ourselves, but our competence comes from God. He has made us competent.
>
> 2 Corinthians 3:4–6

The word *competent* here in the original Greek language is the word *hikanos*, and it can mean the following: sufficient, fit in character, able, good—and, drumroll please—*enough*. Can you believe it? Competent can be translated as the word *enough*. Let's look at that same passage again using the word *enough*.

> Not that we are *enough* in ourselves . . . but being *enough* comes from God. He has made us *enough*.

To make this point clear, Paul goes on to tell his readers that they are like jars of clay, ordinary clay, so that the power will never be confused with people, but it will always be evidence of God in people (2 Corinthians 4).

Lord help us! We have been duped!

- We have come far from the beginning of God's original plan.
- We have become slick, polished, and poised.
- We have learned how to be depressed, discontent, and insecure.
- We have become ashamed of who we are, if we are not perfect.
- We have come far from the truth, so we learn to hide and believe lies.
- Perfection is the lie, performance is the lifestyle, and depression, insecurity, discontent, and fear are the outcome.

We have been lied to. According to Scripture, we were never meant to be enough! We can be freed from the trap set out for us by embracing the reality of Christ being enough in and through us. Isn't that good news? All this time struggling with not being enough, hanging on to all those old messages, when the real truth is that it was never God's plan for us to be enough.

So, in striving to be enough, we are striving against the will and plan of God. We may still "feel" not enough in certain situations or relationships, but we must trust that he makes us enough. We can learn to press through our old feelings. Getting a spiritual perspective can set us free and enable us to walk through the dysfunction in our thinking to the other side, even stronger than we were before.

When the liar hisses, and believe me, he will, it might sound something like "Oh . . . look at you, who do you think you are? You will never measure up, you will never be enough." We can come right back with truth: "No kidding, bozo, I'm not enough—never have been, never will be, but Christ is enough in me, and he makes me enough. I'm standing in truth, so get lost, you liar!"

As I maneuvered through the new territory of a broken and imperfect life, I had to learn something new. Christ is in me. I am enough in him.

Will you lean into the truth with me?

We can be set free.

We don't have to feel bad about not being enough. Instead, we can try something new. We can embrace the truth that Christ is enough and he lives within us. Are you listening?

He is calling . . .

Come to me, my Spirit lives in you, and I am enough.

Come to me with all your old messages and negative perceptions.

Come to me with all your insecurities.

Come to me with who you really are, how you really feel, what you really believe.

Come out of your hiding and learn to live freely and fully in me.

For Further Reflection

1. Do you, as a woman, relate to the words *not enough*? If so, why?
2. What defines you? Is it your looks, your title, your accomplishments? Is it shame, your failures, your inadequacies? Or is it the woman of the heart?

3. Read Galatians 4:3, 8–9. What basic principles or belief system was part of your programming in the past? Do your core beliefs about yourself, your life, and God line up with biblical truth or do they resemble leftover thinking from your past?

4. Have you ever been trapped by the unspoken call to be pretty, perfect, and polished as a woman? If so, has this followed you into the church community? What within this ideal could be a potential trap for you as a believer today?

5. Read 2 Corinthians 3:5. What does Christ being "enough" mean to you? Have you ever been tempted with self-rejection because you were disappointed with who you are, because you did not think you were good enough? How can this verse begin to set you free?

3

No More Hiding

When Love Whispers My Name

Don't let me hide myself from you, God. Give me the courage to open my heart to you in truth and honesty.

Tim Hansel

I have a little white dog named Bubba. It's an unusual name for a fluffy bichon frise, but that's what the kids named him, and we're sticking to it. I love Bubba. He brings me joy that I never expected. As a new pet owner, I was surprised that I missed him during the day when I was away from him.

I can remember many times being excited to see him when I returned home—and it was mutual. He had a favorite spot on top of our sofa in the living room looking out over the yard through a large picture window. As I came up the walk I would see him with his big white plume tail wagging. Oh, he was so happy to see me—until he heard the key unlock the door. Then something strange would happen. I would open the door and start my regular "dog talk." "Hey, Bubbs, I'm home! Where is my Bubbie?" I fully expected him to leap off his perch on the sofa and come bounding toward me, but instead he would find a place to hide.

The first few times I didn't get it. Here I was loving him, missing him, and just wanting to be with him—and instead of coming to me, he would hide under the sofa. Well, at least he *tried* hiding under the sofa. Have you ever seen a bichon? They can't get under a sofa—Bubba just thought he could. His tail gave him away every time. While his head and upper half were buried in secret, his fluffy little backside and big feather tail would be in clear view.

As soon as I dropped my things in the entry, I would go over to the sofa and get him out. I would try talking some sense into my silly dog. "Bubba, what's wrong with you? Why are you hiding? I just want to see you! I miss Bubba and love Bubba!" Over time I began to realize that Bubba would hide because during the time I was away, he had gotten into some form of mischief. He either had an accident in the house, chewed something he shouldn't, or pulled food out of the pantry leaving a trail of suspect wrappers in his path. He knew what he'd done—so he would hide from me.

I got to thinking how similar I am to Bubba. I don't hide under couches, but I sometimes think I can hide from God. I haven't understood how much my heavenly Father values me, and so I hide because I believe that I am bad and unworthy of his love. Certainly unworthy of his time or attention. But just like Bubba, I can't really hide. Truth is, though we think we are tucked away, God sees us and always keeps us in his clear view. Silly me, hiding from the God who loves me and just wants to be with me!

Do you ever find yourself hiding from God?

About five years ago I met a woman who would soon become a fixture in my life. During the craziness of Vacation Bible School, a young mother sought me out at the church—not an easy task with hundreds of kids filing through cramped hallways, but Carly was determined to find me. She needed someone to talk to, and since I was the director of women's ministries, she thought I might be a good place to start. We met by bumping into each other in the hallway. After some polite "excuse me's," she asked if we could talk.

In the midst of the chaos we managed to find a little corner to have a private conversation. I was immediately taken by the sadness that characterized her beautiful brown eyes. She began spilling out her situation through tears and shame, and I realized that this meeting was indeed planned by God. My heart went out to her. We both had been touched by the fire of pain—different circumstances, but familiar heart pain.

She began to paint a picture for me—darling in appearance, perfect little mother of two cute and obedient children. One perfectly put together husband, whom she had been with forever, and a Pottery Barn perfect house. No one would have ever guessed the deep pain that she had been secretly carrying for many years. She cooked, she cleaned, she smiled, and she read her Bible and went to church. Wasn't that supposed to be her insurance policy? Guess not, because life happened.

That week she caught her husband with his hands in the cookie jar of Internet porn. It wasn't his first offense. It made her mad, made her sick to her stomach, and made her true feelings about herself spill out all over the place. Though the main issue at hand was her husband's Internet infidelity, it was obvious the real issue was how she had always viewed herself. Though I'd be hard-pressed to find anything wrong with her appearance, she saw herself as a "rag," and a throwaway one at that. She was breaking before my eyes. But I knew that the old lies had to be demolished so real beauty could come to life within her. Because no matter how beautiful she was on the outside, the inside of her was filled with the uglies. Lies and ugly perceptions about herself and her life haunted her on a daily basis. She thought she was stupid, clumsy, and too fat— though she was barely a size 4.

The Need for a New Heart

I could relate to her pain. Because I had experienced God's faithfulness getting to me and changing me at a deep level, I now wanted to see the miracle of change in her too. Yes, I knew what was ahead of us. There would be many meetings, many tears, lots of prayer, and a few years of feeding her truth—one bite at a time. It was not an overnight, pat answer fix—it was going to be a process. She would have to come out of hiding and be real about her heart pain. God had something new for her.

> I will give you a new heart and put a new spirit in you; I will re-move from you your heart of stone and give you a heart of flesh. . . . You will be my people and I will be your God.
>
> Ezekiel 36:26, 28

God desires to give us a new heart. Think of the contrast of the two types of hearts mentioned:

Heart of stone: dull, heavy, hard, cold, dead.

Heart of flesh: warm, pliable, beating, keeping rhythm, alive.

Carly isn't the only woman who needed a new heart. Over the years I have come across woman after woman who was in need of a new heart and a new start. Coming out of hiding and admitting where we are is not easy but essential. That is what happened one day with a woman named Mary. It was our first meeting. I thought it would be a getting-to-know-you type of appointment, but instead Mary came fully prepared to be transparent and vulnerable. There were no masks and no pretending. Instead she came into my office carrying an index card with well-thought-out words that described her feelings about her life on that Tuesday afternoon. Slowly and deliberately she began to read her penned words to me:

Numb

Depressed

Scared

Paralyzed

Tired

Confused

Sad

Angry

Though these words are not unusual, what is unusual is a woman actually opening up and speaking of an imperfect life while admitting personal failure and pain. Women long for a picture-perfect life. And when it isn't, they become expert at prettying up the picture, because to admit anything else would be to admit they are not perfect, perhaps not spiritual, and certainly less than the other perfect-looking women scurrying around the church. They learn the art of stuffing down the internal wrestling that happens when Christian lives don't match the fairy-tale proportions that we have come to call abundance and blessing. But the truth is, Christ isn't surprised by less-than-perfect people or lives. He is in the business of taking people from broken and bruised to beautiful.

Life happens to each of us, and many things that come our way are not what we had hoped for or planned. We have a need to learn how to live in the reality of Christ even in our darkest and most discouraging moments. I could relate to Mary because her list matched my own almost identically.

I believe that God, through his Son, Jesus, really does have something more for us. I believe that we have been lied to, that we have learned to hide in the pits of our own private pain. But I also believe with everything in me that there is something more, something real, something different. My real life required something different than the path I walked before. I needed the Holy Spirit's power, the touch of a healer, the gentleness of a comforter, and the deliverance of a Savior. I needed a miracle.

> **Miracle**: a remarkable event that seems impossible to explain and is therefore attributed to a supernatural agency.

Scripture says that with God all things are possible. In light of the realities of my life, "all things are possible" sounded a bit miraculous. I had hoped that Jesus would be this kind of miracle in my midst. But as I walked through ordinary days it seemed that a miracle was out of reach.

The Dance of Hiding

People have been hiding for years. Just look at Adam and Eve in the Garden of Eden.

They were created in the image of God, and he had a plan for them. Sin entered the equation, and from then on man and woman began the dance of hiding.

Hiding is empty—a far cry from the life of abundance and freedom that God created us for. Simon Tugwell wrote, "We hide what we know or feel ourselves to be behind some kind of appearance which we hope will be more pleasing . . . and in time we may even come to forget we are hiding."[1]

Wanting to be well-liked and looking for love, I learned from a young age how to hide. I didn't hide in closets or behind corners, but I learned to hide who I was behind a facade of who I thought I should be. I learned to play out life in a game of pretend. Soon after becoming a Christian I also hid behind being busy, useful, and important to God and others.

Maybe you know that dance too.

But do you know the greater story about your life? If you did, you wouldn't be hiding, covered in shame, afraid to come out. Instead of being like Bubba trying to stuff himself away, you would be running to the front door of the house when the Father comes home, jumping into his arms, understanding that he just wants to be with you.

And that's what I'd be doing too—if I fully understood the love of God at heart level.

I Want My Father Back

A few years ago Sandy came into my office at the church for some much-needed encouragement. I had never met her before. I sat and listened as she poured out sorrow upon sorrow, when all of a sudden she blurted out, "Debbie, I just want my father back!"

"Did your father pass away too?" I asked.

Sighing, she began to paint a picture for me. "No, I mean, I just want my father back, Jesus, that father."

"Well, where did he go?" I asked, now very curious.

"You see, I accepted Christ when I was in college. Everything was great. I was involved in campus ministry and was growing in my relationship with God daily. He was my everything. It was the happiest time of my life." She smiled as her memory brought her back to that time.

"Well, what happened?" I asked.

"Oh, I met Roy. He was six years older than me, wise beyond his years, drop-dead gorgeous, and already established in life. I guess you could say that Roy became like my father—he loved me and took care of me, a real sugar daddy." She giggled at the thought of it now.

"Roy and I married, and he became my everything. All love was focused on Roy, and Jesus was no longer the object of my affection, because Roy filled that spot. Jesus was moved to a different position; he was still in my life, but now he seemed more like Uncle Jesus." She took a breath, shook her head, and continued.

"Then we started having kids, and I got so infatuated with motherhood and so busy with the children that Jesus got moved in rank again. He became like long-distance-relative Jesus. Still clearly in my life, still one of my loves, but not in my daily world. You know, just like the pictures on a refrigerator of relatives you don't regularly see. You think of them, you love them, you smile when you see their Kodak faces. You would jump on a plane if they really needed something. But for all intents and purposes, they are far away, removed, and not part of your everyday life. That's what Christ has become to me—a long-distance relative!"

Now crying, she continued, "But my life is falling apart. My children have left the nest, I was just diagnosed with breast cancer, my husband is off on his Harley enjoying his midlife crisis, and I am empty. I have no peace, no purpose, and just want to get back to the place I was in the beginning—where Jesus was my Father. Debbie, do you think it's possible to start over after so many years of mediocre Christian living?"

I took a deep breath and silently asked God to give me wisdom, words, and sensitivity to her situation. Her words tugged at the strings of my own heart, because I knew firsthand about mediocre living. Together we began to talk about starting over and putting Jesus first again. We talked about his love and how he just longs to be with us, to pull us back to his side. It was this love we were created for.

I don't think Sandy is much different than many of us. We come to Christ and flit happily through the honeymoon period of our faith. It is the best time. Why? Because our focus is so pure. We are connecting to Christ for the first time. It's exciting, exhilarating, and we just can't get enough of Jesus or his love. Then something happens.

We get busy. We either get busy with life, our families, or with serving in the church. We are such a busy people, just like the church in Ephesus. It's not that we have bad motives, we just don't realize how far we begin moving from the love relationship that we were created for.

What a powerful illustration she gave me that day. Jesus the long-distance relative rather than Jesus the lover of our soul. Jesus our beloved, the God who longs to be our first love, relegated to the bottom rung of the ladder.

Learning to Rely on Love

Do you remember what it was like when you first believed in Christ? Can you picture the day, the season, your age? Where were you emotionally then? What life circumstances brought you to the place of wanting to believe?

This was the beginning of your love story.

Maybe the gospel of grace never moved from your head to heart. Perhaps it never penetrated the part of you that would make it real enough to base your whole life on. If so, perhaps you need to "start over." It doesn't matter how long you've been a believer, or even if you served and led ministries. A beautiful thing happens when we come out of hiding and decide that we desire something more—something deeper. He meets us at this place and begins unraveling the lies and making his truth our new reality. Take a look at this verse and read it a few times. Try reading it out loud.

And so we know and rely on the love God has for us.

1 John 4:16

I don't think we have trouble with the first part of this verse—knowing. It's the second part of the verse—relying—that is a bit iffy. We all know in our heads about Jesus and his love. We have heard about it, we have sung about it, we recognize that it is supposed to be true. But we need the second part of that verse, because we need to take that truth as our own—becoming convinced it is personal enough to depend on it.

The word *know* in the original Greek is the word *ginosko*, which means to find out, recognize, understand, keep in mind, realize, or remember. The word *rely* in the original is *pistuo*, which means to believe in, to put faith in, to trust in, to take as the word of truth. Can you see the difference?

56

One is the head knowing and finding out *about* God's love, and the other is the heart learning to put complete trust in and take it in personally as absolute truth. The second part of the verse is where we learn to actively live in God's love, and then the truth of love travels from head to heart. (We will look at practical ways to walk this out in later chapters.) This truth is our very foundation, the base that all else is built upon.

Over the course of time I began to learn the beauty of truth making its home within me. I have experienced the difference. Oh, the serpent still hisses, but truth stands up to prevail. For I am convinced now that God himself wants to have relationship with me—yes, me, one who flops and fails. And I write this book because I know that he desires a very personal relationship with you too. This relationship was meant to be your reality and change your perspective.

Perhaps you have been a Christian for a long time and have known intimacy of relationship with him, but now Jesus is more like your uncle or long-distance relative. Possibly you are in a very connected relationship with Christ, but all the information in your head has not been lived out in life transformation yet. Or maybe you have never known Christ in an up-close-and-personal way but are just waiting for something to click. Keep seeking, because you will find him. Take a breath, get real about where you are in life, say a prayer, and get ready to walk in a new dance of love. By the way, there is no fear in love, so if you are struggling with issues that are rooted in fear, take heart—God wants to teach you the new freeing dance steps of his love for you. His love, as it becomes your reality, drives out fear.

If you had a personal appointment with God today, what words would be on your index card list to lay out before him? What would describe the "real you"? Forget the crowds, culture, or others' expectations—instead, search your own heart and come out of hiding and lay your list before him now. He will meet you when you come to him. This is the first step. We must come out of hiding. We must get real if we are going to be in relationship with the living God.

So take off the masks, stop the clichés. It's time to come forward. Just like I would come home saying, "Bubbie, come out, where are you?" the lover of our souls says, *Honey, come out, I just want to love you. I've missed you all day. Where have you been?*

Slowly, as we begin to come out of our place of shame and hiding, we learn the truth about us and the truth about God. If we listen, we will hear him whisper our name. It probably won't be audible, but it will be a whisper of the heart.

Jif Camsters, the King of the Hamsters

When my youngest son was eight years old, all he wanted for his birthday was a hamster. Because I don't like hamsters or anything remotely resembling a rodent, I told him to wish for something else. But a dear, sweet relative (does the name Grandma explain why he got what he wished for?) gave Cameron what his eight-year-old heart wanted the most—a hamster. So Jif came to live with our family. Jif was named affectionately after Cam's favorite food at the time—Jif peanut butter. For the love of my son, I went along with it, but I wasn't crazy about the idea of our new addition.

In my opinion, there are two things wrong with having a hamster in the home—they stink, and they make too much noise at night. I know the kids promise to clean the cage, but really, do they? Well, let's just say, when they don't hold up their end of the bargain, things get stinky. Then there is the problem with the squeaky wheel. Today you can purchase quiet plastic hamster habitats. But back then, there was just that old squeaky metal wheel—and it was noisy all night long.

I never realized I was such a light sleeper until we had Jif. Night after night he ran his wheel . . . squeak, squeak, squeak . . . ugh!

By now my life had taken a different shape. I was remarried, and together my husband and I had four children. We were a few years into our new blended family when Jif came to live with us. The two girls were sound asleep in their room, my two boys were asleep in the room with Jif, and my husband was sleeping soundly in our room—all while I was wide awake! I tossed and turned, put the pillow over my head, but still . . . squeak, squeak, squeak. I wanted to scream.

After three consecutive nights of very little sleep I was ready to lose it! You know the saying, "If Mama's not happy, nobody's happy!" Well, this Mama was clearly not happy. In fact, I was worse than unhappy, I was over the edge. Finally in my frustration I sprang out of bed at one in the morning, threw on my robe, and went stomping down the hall to the boys' room, the place Jif called home sweet home.

I yanked off the towel that covered his cage and did what any mother does when there is a problem. I got in his face! That's right; I got eye to eye with a hamster and began to try reasoning with him.

"Jif, look at yourself. You are running and running and running, and you aren't getting anywhere. Can't you see that this wheel-running stuff is a dead end? Where are you going? Do you ever wonder where you're going, Jif? You stupid hamster, just stop! Please just stop running!"

But the more I spoke to Jif, the faster he ran, looking straight ahead, lost in his own little hamster world. For a split second I almost snapped and tossed him out the window—but I came to my senses. I soon realized that no amount of persuasion on my part was going to make a difference; in fact, when I spoke to Jif it seemed to stimulate him and make him run even faster. So I gave up and went back down the hall to my room, threw the covers over my head, and began to cry. And I'm not talking little tears; I'm talking ugly snot crying tears. My level of frustration surprised even me. Obviously there was more to this than just a hamster.

As hot tears stung my eyes, I thought of where my life had taken me over the past few years. I thought about how my life had broken apart, and how I had tried to put all the pieces back together again. But I had to admit I was like Humpty Dumpty. All the king's horses and all the king's men couldn't put me together again. Goodness knows I tried to find the glue in a new relationship, new family, new job, and a new neighborhood. But instead of putting me back together, I just became stuck. I needed the King himself. I had tried all other resources and still found myself crying in the middle of the night over a stupid hamster. It clearly was not the hamster—it was me. My life was a wreck!

There between sniffling and silence, under my blankets, God spoke to me. It wasn't an audible conversation, but one that I heard clearly in the depths of my heart. It was a true defining moment, one that would begin changing my life forever.

"Debbie, you are just like Jif."

What? Just like Jif? A hamster? What do you mean, Lord? I'm fat, smelly, and obnoxious?

"Debbie, you are just like Jif because you run. 'Better, better, better' is the song of your soul. You run and run and run and are getting nowhere. You look straight ahead, focusing on your own little problems, in your own little world. You get so wrapped up in yourself and fixing things that you forget about everything else. Did you ever wonder where you are going—and what the purpose is to

your running? Can't you see that you are on the wheel of perfection and performance, and this wheel isn't really going anywhere? Why don't you stop your running and stop trying to prove yourself? Can you stop trying to be 'enough'? Just rest, my precious daughter. Rest in who you are as my own . . . just come and learn to rest in me. It's in me that you find real life. I will help you discover your purpose, and I will enable you to live off the wheel."

I was then reminded of the words of Christ in the book of Matthew:

Come to me, all you who are weary and burdened, and I will give you rest.

Matthew 11:28

Those words became a direct call to me personally.

"Come to me, Debbie, I can see you are tired, burdened, and worn out. I can see your broken heart, your shattered dreams, and your feelings of worthlessness. I see how you have lost your way, not knowing who you are or if your life has real purpose. I will give you rest from all the perfection and expectations that you have piled upon yourself for a lifetime. I will give you rest from trying to be somebody special, rest from trying to be better, rest from trying to get yourself together. Yes, I will give you rest, my precious one. I will restore you, be the glue that binds you, and I will show you the way."

I had to admit the truth. My life was defined by the wrong messages, and my actions were driven by those messages. For many years, as a Christian, I talked as if everything depended on the Lord and lived like it all depended on me. I was living a mixed message.

Whew! No wonder I was tired. I lacked God's perspective. I was trying to *be* somebody special, and until that night I didn't understand that I already *was* somebody special—not because of me but because of the God who created me. Oh, the father of lies did not want me figuring this out. He did not want me answering the call to come closer to Jesus. The liar didn't want me to be defined by truth—by love, grace, and acceptance. Of course not, he wanted to keep me bound up in self, insecurity, and fear.

That night under the covers I got the message loud and clear. Jesus had the better way. I was to return to the place of love, learn what that meant for me personally, and be freed by his thoughts and truths about me. It would be a step-by-step journey to freedom. Listen to how Eugene Peterson describes the Matthew 11:28 verse in the Message:

Are you tired? Worn out? Burned out on religion? Come to me. Get away with me and you'll recover your life. I'll show you how to take a real rest. Walk with me and work with me—watch how I do it. Learn the unforced rhythm of grace. I won't lay anything heavy or ill-fitting on you. Keep company with me and you'll learn to live freely and lightly.

I was going to learn to live freely and lightly? Me, Debbie, who always thought she was not enough, was going to recover her life and learn the unforced rhythm of grace?

A. W. Tozer wrote,

To most people God is an inference, not a reality. He is a deduction from evidence which they consider adequate, but He remains personally unknown to the individual. For millions of Christians God is not more real than He is to the non-Christian. Over against all cloudy vagueness stands the clear scriptural doctrine that God can be known in personal experience. A loving Personality dominates the Bible.[2]

When we begin to grasp that God is not like some taskmaster making his list and checking it twice but rather a loving Personality, we can move into a different kind of relationship with him. One of love and trust.

It took me some time, but eventually I came out from my hiding spot and stepped off the wheel. I learned that the place of self-protection that I had formed around me didn't protect me at all. Truth is, it caused me more pain than I realized. It was time to get real, bare naked before the God who created me—stripped from pretense and performance, surrendering perfection and my future. This was my time to start over. This was my day to be made new. Some may guide us to God and others may help us understand God. But there is no one who does the work of God, for only God can heal us. The freest woman in the world is the one who has an open heart, a broken spirit, and a new direction to travel. It's time to come out of hiding and step into healing.

To come simply means . . . to move toward something.

Oswald Chambers said, "The attitude necessary for you to come to Him is one where your will has made the determination to let go of everything and deliberately commit it all to Him." He also said, "The questions that truly matter in life are remarkably few, and they are all answered by these words— 'Come to Me.' "[3]

He is calling us. Can you hear him saying, "Come"?

Come out from your hiding spot. I just want to love you.
Come with your secrets and shame; I already know about your life.
Come and listen, I want to speak the truth of grace to you.
Come surrender so you can be set free.

For Further Reflection

1. If you had an appointment with God today, what would be the words on your list to present to him?

2. Do you ever find yourself hiding behind appearances? Or do you ever find yourself like Jif on the wheel, running and lost in your own little world of details and troubles?

3. What are some of the things you did at first in your relationship with Christ? Why do you suppose those are things we need to return to?

4. Do the words "Come to me" sound too simplistic to you? What would it mean for you to actually come to Jesus with your life today? What would that look like? According to Matthew 11:28, what would that change?

4

His

Embracing the Truth of Who i Am

Remember, He has identified you as his own.

Ephesians 4:30 NLT

When my Stepford Christian life came crashing down, I found myself wondering, "Who am I?" My identity was shaken as I lost the title of "Mrs.," stepped down from ministry, and began to shuffle children back and forth. I felt broken, empty, and lost. It wasn't a pretty sight. In fact, there was nothing pretty, perfect, or polished left of me. I was raw, rough, and riding on an emotional roller coaster.

I spent the next few years trying to fix myself by finding new things to fill me. Like that song "Haven't Got Time for the Pain," I was trying with all my might to make the pain go away. And even though I started a brand-new life, pain ended up finding me. Before long I found myself slowly falling into a pit of despair—down, down, down. I sank further and deeper than I had ever been. I ended up clinically depressed.

When all I could think of was driving into a wall or jumping off a bridge, I swallowed my pride and at the suggestion of the counselor I was seeing went to the doctor for medical help. He gave me a prescription for antidepressants. I skipped to my car, little white bag in hand, with joyful anticipation of the miracle waiting for me when I took these new little pills. But hope was short lived.

Like all drugs, there is fine print and cautions in the pharmaceutical leaflet. When serious side effects began within the first week, I was back to the doctor's office.

My doctor examined me and then jotted something in my file. He looked at me sternly as he said, "There are some people who can't take antidepressant medications, and you are one of those people." On the verge of tears, I managed to mumble, "Well, what am I going to do? Is there something else we can try?" And, as if his voice was stalled in slow motion, I heard him say, "Well, I'm afraid you are just going to have to get yourself together." *Get . . . yourself . . . together . . .*

What? Get myself together? Is this guy crazy? Now I was angry. Dr. No-Bedside-Manner stole my joy, my hope, and my chance of getting out of this pit. If I could get myself together I wouldn't be here groveling for drugs at a doctor's office! I just wanted to slap the man, but instead I left the office and sat in my car crying so hard that I thought I would die right there. The black cloud that covered me seemed to be keeping me at arm's length from freedom. It was clear I needed more help! But now the help I thought I needed was gone—unavailable to me.

Between crying and wiping my nose, I began to have a little talk with the Lord. *Oh God, it's not fair. My life is a disaster. What am I going to do now? I've tried everything that I can think of trying. Now what? I'm losing it, Lord. Can't you see I'm losing it! I have two little boys to raise, a new family to fit into, a new husband to please. I'm an absolute mess . . . and Lord . . . did you hear me? I'm losing it . . .*

A verse from the Bible began trickling into my mind. "He sent forth his Word and healed them." I didn't know where that was in the Bible or where it was coming from, but over and over I kept hearing the message softly and tenderly. *He sends his Word to heal his people.*

I must admit I was less than impressed with the thought—truth is, I was downright cynical. I was in my own real life pit, and I must admit I thought something like, *Yeah, right . . . been there, done that before. I'm in need of help—real help.*

That very afternoon I received from an old friend a card that had a passage from Psalm 40 on the front of it. My eyes locked into the miry clay and the slimy pit that this passage spoke of. Just like the psalmist, I was in a pit, and I began to hope that I too could be pulled up and out of it.

> I waited patiently for the LORD;
>> he turned to me and heard my cry.
> He lifted me out of the slimy pit,
>> out of the mud and mire;
> he set my feet on a rock
>> and gave me a firm place to stand.
> He put a new song in my mouth,
>> a hymn of praise to our God.
> Many will see and fear
>> and put their trust in the LORD.
>
> Psalm 40:1–3

A small glimmer of hope began to take root as I read and reread the account of David's deliverance from the pit. It was obvious to me—I was in a pit. I had cried out to the Lord—and maybe, just maybe, he would give me a firm place to stand. And maybe, just maybe, a new song would rise up from deep within and my broken life would someday bring blessing. It was the beginning of hope.

Maybe you have been stuck in the hole of loss and confusion. Or maybe your pit is a life that has been interrupted by problems, pain, and unexpected things. Like Carly, maybe your pit has been deep feelings of inferiority, insecurity, and shame. In any case—a pit is a pit, and you need God's hand to pull you up and out of it.

He promises to do just that.

He turns to us and hears us when we call to him.

He lifts us out of the pit.

He sets us in a new, firm place.

He puts a new song in our mouth.

He gives us the joy to praise him.

Unfortunately we often choose that pitiful pit instead of the spacious, firm place that God can take us to. We know the pit; we've learned how to live there. We might not be happy, but we are comfortable with our pain, our insecurities, and our fears. It's almost as if we don't know any better. We put on our little Stepford faces, smiling and saying everything is just fine. By the way, have you heard the acronym of fine?

Freaked Out

Insecure

Neurotic

Emotional

Transformed by Love

Over the past few years I have watched from a distance as a friend of mine was transformed by love. She married late in life, at a time when she thought she'd be single forever. Over the years, as a single woman who had given up on love, she did little to attract the attention of a man—and basically became a bit frumpy in appearance and attitude. But when she least expected it, her prince came waltzing into her life, loving her just as she was—frumpy and all. He swept her off her feet—physically, emotionally, and spiritually. Before long they began to plan a new life together, and slowly she began to transform—the whole caterpillar into a butterfly thing.

Love gave her a new confidence. It wasn't a boastful, ugly confidence but a gentle and beautiful assurance of her position as one who was loved. During the dating phase she radically changed from a woman who was average to a complete and stunning beauty. No one required the change, the change happened as she responded to love.

The other day we were catching up with each other, and I commented on how she always looked so beautiful, even just running to the grocery store. She smiled and winked. "Well, I'm representing my love. I am part of him, now I have his name, and I want to reflect him well."

The very thought of her being identified with and being a reflection of her new husband reminded me of the truth that says we are identified with Christ—and our lives are a reflection of him. Sadly, we don't always take God's love for us to heart. We question it, doubt it, apply conditions to it. But when this love becomes our new reality, our new belief system, we do change. We experience the caterpillar to butterfly thing too. Our spirit begins to soar. No longer in search for extraordinary, we begin to enjoy, appreciate, and love the ordinary moments of each day . . . just being his.

Reshaped as His Woman

Like a potter shaping a beautiful pot on the wheel, the Lord God shapes and reshapes us according to his design.

This is the word that came to Jeremiah from the LORD: "Go down to the potter's house, and there I will give you my message." So I went down to the potter's house, and I saw him working at the wheel. But the pot he was shaping from the clay was marred in his hands; so the potter formed it into another pot, shaping it as seemed best to him. Then the word of the LORD came to me: "O house of Israel, can I not do with you as the potter does?" declares the LORD. "Like clay in the hand of the potter, so are you in my hand."

Jeremiah 18:1–6

The reshaping of the clay on the wheel is part of the process of us being transformed into something new and different. We are being worked on by the powerful hands of the master potter. He is the potter and we are the clay. We are being shaped on his wheel—spinning round and round, while he is faithfully creating us into his design. But there are times when he pushes the clay down because the shape the pot is taking isn't quite right—much like the heart demolition. This new shaping will bring us into all that the Master has designed for us—as his.

Remember it is his love that is forming us. Where we are marred, he begins anew, shaping us as seems best to him. This potter, this God who is above everything, is the same God who wants to be our entire reality—our new vision, our new heart, the new Spirit within us.

Brennan Manning speaks of this miracle. "Is this miracle enough for anybody? Or has the thunder of 'God loved the world so much' been so muffled by the roar of religious rhetoric that we are deaf to the word that God could have tender feelings for us?"[1]

Many Hats

As women we have so many roles—and the hats we wear are endless! It's easy for women to get stuck in an identity crisis, basing who we are solely on what we do or who we are associated with. Our names may change if we marry; our titles may change in the workplace; we may move across the country. It's amazing to think that God knows who we are in each episode of the drama of our lives, even when we don't recognize ourselves.

When I gave birth to my first son, I wished for a "how-to" book. But the hospital didn't send me home with a nice little booklet on how to be a mother. Every mom becomes a nurse, a cheerleader, a chauffeur, a policewoman. And even if you're not a mother, you probably wear hats like friend, personal shopper, working woman, and home accountant. It's enough to make your head spin, isn't it? But regardless of how tired you are, how many carpools you have driven in today, how many messes you have cleaned up, how many bills you have paid, and how many kids you have had to reprimand, at the end of the day you are still a woman—and women spend their lives wearing many hats.

No wonder it's hard to get off the hamster wheel! No wonder we get lost and forget who we really are! It's easy to see how we forget that God loves us—we are too busy rushing about to remember much of anything!

I've illustrated this at speaking engagements by putting on props representing all the different hats a woman wears. I would start explaining the different hats we wear by layering things beginning with a wedding veil, apron, cleaning gloves, baby bear wrapped in blankets—then different things representing different parts of our lives as women. But before I ever made this presentation to a group, I practiced by trying on all the props in my bedroom behind closed doors.

It was a Friday afternoon, and that night I was to speak at a young moms' group. The kids were still at school and I was home practicing. I was layered with things—veil, tiara, apron, dusting glove, a bear wrapped in a swaddling blanket, a stethoscope around my neck, a magic wand in one hand and a pom-pom poking out from the other. As if this weren't enough, I had a white see-through negligee robe draped over my shoulders.

Knock, knock. *Oh, the kids must be home from school,* I thought while making my way to the bedroom door. Completely oblivious to how I must have looked, I flung the door open, happy to see them. "Hi, guys!" I said as if everything was normal. But I didn't even closely resemble a normal mom at three in the afternoon!

My ten-year-old son and his friend just stood there staring at me in shock. My son began to snicker while his stunned friend questioned my identity. "Mrs. Alsdorf?" And before I could answer he ran down the stairs and out of the house as fast as his little soccer legs could take him—just like he had seen a ghost or something equally as scary. He never came back.

Can you just imagine the dinner conversation at his house that night? I wish I could have been a fly on those walls. I'm sure I was portrayed as some crackpot old lady, playing dress up with magic wands, bridal veils, a queen's tiara, and a baby bear! I still laugh just thinking of it. I can only imagine what his parents thought.

Women always get a good laugh at the props too—probably because we can all relate. But not knowing *who* we are and *whose* we are is no laughing matter. We spend so much of our lives being identified by titles, achievements, and associations that we forget who we really are. And though each role is definitely part of our lives, we run into trouble when that role is our only identification of who we are—because the truest thing about us then goes unrecognized for years.

You see, all those hats and roles represent things we do, not who we are. When living for others—our spouses, our children, our bosses, or our friends—we can lose ourselves when any of those relationships change. Given the fact that relationships always change, we are setting ourselves up for heartache. But when our identity becomes rooted in God and the fact that we have been created for his purposes, we never lose ourselves when things change. We just move on to the next season of the journey with him—identity solidly intact, realizing that our life revolves around a bigger picture.

Let's look at the truth:

Who are you?

You are a child of God.

You have been created by him and for him.

He has equipped you for every good work.

Every gift has come from the Father.

He knows everything about you.

He says his work is good (that's you).

He loves you enough to lay down his own life for your freedom.

He declares you as valuable.

He is committed to providing all your needs.

He has a design—plan, intent, and purpose—for your life.

Whose are you?

El Roi—the God who sees

El Elyon—the God most high

El Shaddai—the all-sufficient one

Jehovah Jireh—the provider

Jehovah Rapha—the healer

Jehovah Shalom—my peace

Jehovah Raah—my shepherd

Jehovah Nissi—my banner

Given the truth, we have two choices:

1. Create our own purpose and identity.
2. Accept the identity and purpose God has already given us.

In order to have a strong foundation with your confidence placed firmly in God, you must know who you are (created by God) and whose you are (belonging to God). This is foundational. Part of getting real with God is coming to the place of admitting that our foundation has not been as firm as we thought, and we must now lay all of ourselves down in surrender.

Proverbs 31—the Missing Piece

The woman in Proverbs 31 had a mile-long list of things she did too. But there is a verse that I think we sometimes overlook—and it gives a clue into who she was, not just what she did. In verse 22 it says that she "does her own sewing, and everything she wears is beautiful" (NCV). Then verse 25 speaks of a different kind of clothing: "She is clothed with strength and dignity and she laughs without fear of the future" (NLT). One was her outward appearance—the woman everyone sees. The other was who she was on the inside—the woman of the heart.

Can you laugh with no fear of the future? None of us knows the future. There are so many things that are not within the realm of our control, so what kind of woman would be able to laugh or rejoice over the unknowns in life?

The proverb ends by saying she was a woman who feared the Lord. I guess we could say she knew *whose* she was! She embraced the sovereignty of the Almighty the same way we now need to embrace the tender love of Christ for us. When we understand his love for us, fear begins to be replaced by an assurance of his presence with us. Our longing to belong is met with understanding that we do belong—to him.

Somewhere along the way, as I was intentionally starting over, I decided that I wanted that kind of God-confidence. The first step toward that kind of confidence meant that I had to get real with God and admit that though I sometimes acted like I had full confidence in God, I never did—or maybe I only experienced it in fleeting moments. But now I wanted it—I wanted to breathe it, live it, and find myself in it. I wanted desperately to know God in a way like I never had—up close and personal. It was becoming clearer and clearer that I had to go back to basics. Though I hadn't previously spent much time thinking about *who* I belonged to, now was the time to let it sink into every part of me. And as truth began to penetrate me, I found healing.

This verse in Deuteronomy became important for my rebuilding:

> For you are a people [a woman] holy to the LORD your God. The
> LORD your God has chosen you out of all the peoples [women] on
> the face of the earth to be his people [his woman], his treasured

possession. The LORD did not set his affection on you and choose you because you were more numerous than other peoples, for you were the fewest of all peoples. But it was because the LORD loved you.

Deuteronomy 7:6–8

GOD, your God, chose you out of all the people on the Earth for himself as a cherished, personal treasure. GOD wasn't attracted to you and didn't choose you because you were big and important—the fact is, there was almost nothing to you. He did it out of sheer love.

Deuteronomy 7:6–8 Message

Have you ever thought of yourself as God's treasured possession? What about his cherished personal treasure?

God's Word puts the stamp of approval in my heart, moving me to believe that I really am authentically his. This new definition makes all the difference in my daily life. Remember that what defines us, at the core of our hearts, is what drives us.

Oswald Chambers says, "To say 'I am not my own,' is to have reached a high point in my spiritual stature. . . . This is evidenced by the deliberate giving up of myself to another Person through a sovereign decision, and that person is Jesus Christ."[2]

Transformation Takes Time

These days I smile when I get emails from Carly. She always signs them, "His Carly." But living by a new definition didn't come easily for her. Carly had trouble believing that she simply was his, and certainly had trouble grasping the truth that she was God's treasure. She likened herself to a puppy getting crumbs from under the table—never imagining *she* could be seated at the table. As she began to grasp the Father's love, the flower of Carly unfolded petal by petal over time. She just needed to be reminded of truth—over and over again. Slowly what was real according to God's view of her began to sink in. Like Carly, we all need to be reminded too.

Remembering the Truth

Do you ever walk into a room looking for something and then wonder why you are in there? Maybe it's age, or just that I have too much going on. Whatever the reason, I need sticky notes, a daily calendar, and other tangibles to remind me of things that are important.

I also need reminders of key core biblical truths—things like, I am his, and I am loved. One minute I'm sure of these truths and have peace, the next minute I am worrying again. I often act like I am fending for myself and on my own, without a God who calls me his. I want to remember the truth of who I am and whose I am in the good times, the bad times, and most especially in the middle of regular days. That's why for the past several years, an engraved Tiffany-style bracelet has dangled from my wrist to help remind me of who I am and whose I am. One side of a heart-shaped charm reads "His" and the other "1973."

I can still remember the day I picked up my newly engraved bracelet at our local mall. The clerk polished the silver and then smiled sweetly as she said, "Oh, this must be the year you met your husband." I took a deep breath and burst her romantic bubble by saying, "No, it's actually the year that I received Jesus Christ as my Savior and Lord."

"Bye-bye now," the clerk said nervously. "Have a nice day." She couldn't get me out of her store quickly enough!

As I look back over the past thirty-four years of being a Christian I wish that early on someone had sat me down and told me the truth about my new life in Christ.

I wish I had understood that this newness actually changed my identity from someone who had to work things out on her own to a new creation whom God was living in and working in. It's easy to see how we as Christians don't live based on who we really are but instead on whom we appear to be. This is living, at best, with a false reality.

Author Robert McGee puts it this way:

> Some secular psychologists focus on self-worth with a goal of simply feeling good about ourselves. A biblical self-concept, however, goes far beyond that limited perspective. It is an accurate perception of ourselves, God and others based on the truths of God's Word. An accurate, biblical self-concept contains both strength and humility, both sorrow over sin and joy about forgiveness, a deep sense of our need for God's grace and a deep sense of the reality of God's grace.[3]

I needed a deep sense of the reality of God's grace and love for me—so did Carly, and so did Mary when she came into my office with her list of troubled thoughts and feelings. We all need to understand that we have value assigned by God. Our value is secured by Christ and not dependent on our abilities or on the love or acceptance of others. Our value is not based on picket-fence lives and fairy-tale endings. Our value rests in the God who created us. He is the only one who knows us completely and is able to fulfill us from a deeper place than we have ever known.

In the next section of the book we will explore the core truths that God uses to bring us freedom. These truths can reshape how you think about yourself and begin reaffirming God's desire for intimate relationship with you. Over time the fastening of these truths to my life has totally changed my perspective and helped me out of the pit of my depression into eventual healing. As we continue moving through this journey together you will come to see that the Stepford days are behind you. In exchange you will find a real relationship with the living God, your Creator, who loves you and has a design for your life.

He is still saying, "Come . . ."

Come back to the basics of my love for you.

Come learn to rest in the truth that you are mine.

Come to me for change—a new heart, a new life, a transformed mind.

Come, my daughter, and get real before me, giving me the unedited you.

Come, my treasure, and learn that you are mine.

For Further Reflection

1. Have you ever thought much about the single word *his* and what that means to you and your life?
2. What are some of the hats you've worn as a woman—the roles you have filled? How does the identification as "his" make a difference in your perspective on the way you live out your roles and responsibilities?
3. Read Deuteronomy 7:6. How does it affect you to know that you are God's treasure? Does this knowledge change the way you view yourself, or is it just more "spiritual" talk that amounts to nothing in your real life?
4. How can you begin lining your life and your belief system up to the truth? If you believed the truth about you and your life, could you laugh at the future, as the woman in Proverbs 31 was able to? What is the key to that kind of confidence?

Step 2

Getting Back to Basics

Moving Toward Core Truths That Are Essential for Life Change

He sent forth his word and
healed them.

Psalm 107:20

Each step we walk, each breath we
breathe, we know we are preserved by
God, we know we are accompanied
by God, we know we are ruled by
God; and therefore no matter what
doubts we endure or what accidents
we experience, the Lord will guard us
from every evil, he guards our very
life. We know the truth.

Eugene Peterson

Basics
fundamentals; starting point.

Getting back to basics is returning to the foundational starting point. It's taking a fresh look at the truth in God's Word and learning what it means to read it and digest it. It's about sitting long enough with a nugget of truth that it begins to nourish you, change you, and build in you a new belief system.

It is recognizing that you may have been operating for years on the weak and miserable principles of the world—even as a believer. And it's acknowledging the difference between head information and heart transformation. Transformation requires going back to the simplicity of taking God at his Word—believing with every bit of you that his Word is truth and that only truth sets you free.

This kind of freedom can only be experienced by the person who is not just a hearer or a storer of the Word—but this freedom is experienced by one who is an active participant with God through the response and obedience to his Word.

As God's Word begins to penetrate and cut into the deepest part of your heart, things happen and your life changes. But it doesn't happen overnight. Change happens in incremental movement—baby step by baby step. Real spiritual change requires the foundation of the second step—getting back to basics.

5

Transformed by Truth

Set Free by a New Reality

We have a lot to unlearn. Since most of our problems—and all of our bad habits—didn't develop overnight, it's unrealistic to expect them to go away immediately. It requires the hard work of removal and replacement.

Rick Warren

As I walked through the valley of depression I found solace in the safety of processing with the counselor I was seeing. Together we worked through many things, but both of us came to the realization that there was a part of me that remained stuck. Over and over again I kept remembering the verse I had in my head that day when the doctor told me I couldn't take medications for the depression:

"He sent forth his Word and healed them." Unfortunately, at the time, I discounted what God was trying to tell me.

Instead of taking that verse to heart, I tried to fix everything myself. You know the routine, ladies . . . we sometimes think we are superwomen or something. We try with all our might to fix things. You would think I would have known that my fixing things didn't do the job, because a few years earlier I put my hope once again in the fairy-tale dream—and God would not allow even a new life, new husband, or new career to be the perfect fix.

I longed for someone to make sense out of the pieces of my life. I naively believed that peace would be mine at the start of a new life and new family. I had remarried a wonderful man who had two daughters—with my two sons we were just like the Brady Bunch. But after we said "I do" we soon learned that the Bradys only exist on a Hollywood set or television reruns. The blended family was much more complex and much harder than anything I had ever experienced.

Fixing the circumstances was not the answer; it was much deeper than that. Ultimately, I had to admit that I had built my entire Christian life on the wrong foundation. I began to get the picture of a cake in my mind. In the past, the foundation, the cake, was all about me and my life—it consisted of my marriage, our family, our friends, our ministry—all good things. But, sadly, Jesus was just the sweet icing on the top of the cake, when he was supposed to be the substance—the cake. Then life happened, and the cake blew up! And I was left wondering why I had no hope and felt there was no help for me. Jesus addresses this same idea in Matthew 7:24–27:

> Everyone who hears these words of mine and puts them into practice is like a wise man [or woman] who built his house on the rock. The rain came down, the streams rose, and the winds blew

and beat against that house; yet it did not fall, because it had its foundation on the rock. But everyone who hears these words of mine and does not put them into practice is like a foolish man who built his house on sand. The rain came down, the streams rose, and the winds blew and beat against that house, and it fell with a great crash.

That's it! I fell with a great crash. Why? Because when life happened it found me standing on the flimsy foundation of everything else other than God. Believe me, this revelation surprised even me! I used to think of myself as quite spiritual. In my early years I worked hard for God, doing my best and studying for hours to give women a message—when all along Jesus wanted to be the message alive and living in my heart and life. He wanted to be the cake, the substance, the foundation. Sadly, I realized that I was treating him like the icing, the fluff, the disposable part of the equation.

I was in need of a transformation!

Personal Crisis: Where the Rubber Meets the Road

My all-time favorite devotional is *My Utmost for His Highest* by Oswald Chambers. After years of using it on a daily basis I feel certain that Oswald and I will be on a first-name basis in heaven.

Chambers writes about how a crisis can change us:

Before we choose to follow God's will, a crisis must develop in our lives. This happens because we tend to be unresponsive to God's gentler nudges. He brings us to a place where He asks us to be our utmost for Him and we begin to debate. He then providentially provides a crisis where we have to decide—for or against. That moment becomes a great crossroads in our lives. If a crisis has come to you on any front, surrender your will to Jesus absolutely and irrevocably.[1]

It didn't feel like it at the time, but now I realize the breaking of Debbie was a gift.

It's a gift when someone loves you enough to require the hard thing that will move you into a better place. Believe it or not, the Lord loves us more than anyone could ever begin to. He also knows what it will take to move us to the place that will enable him to shape us into the women he has planned for us to be. He has been working in us and orchestrating details since the day we were conceived and hidden in the secret place of our mother's womb.

When my life crumbled around me, the verse "he sent forth his Word and healed them" just kept finding its way back to my mind. I finally realized I should listen and take it seriously. But I had a twofold problem. First of all, I had no hope that truth could really set me free, and secondly I could not even open my Bible. Just the sight of the leather-bound book sent me reeling.

Oh, what a trap laid out by Satan! I couldn't force myself to read the very thing that could truly set me free.

So what do Christian women do when they have a problem? We go to the phone or we go to God's throne! So I did what I knew to do best at the time; I went to the phone and called my friend Liz.

"Liz, God keeps giving me the same verse over and over again. I think the message he's trying to get through to me is that his Word is going to be my medication since I am unable to take antidepressants."

"Well then, you better get the Word in you several times a day," she said with a laugh.

"Yeah, right! Listen, I have a problem. I'm embarrassed to tell you this, but I can't even look at a Bible, much less read it."

"Hmm . . ." She was thinking, and the silence almost made me crazy. "Okay, here's what you can do. Make a photocopy of Psalm 139 and for now that will be your Bible. Read it several times a day and take it with you everywhere you go."

"Why Psalm 139?" I asked, completely unimpressed with her brainstorm.

"I'm not sure. The Lord will show you. Just do it."

Easy for you to say, I thought as I hung up the phone. But, tired of being in the pit, I was ready to try it. So off to Kinko's I went with my Bible in hand. I copied Psalm 139 onto an 8 by 11 sheet of paper. I folded it up and carried it with me everywhere I went. This was going to be serious business. As serious as taking medication, antibiotics, or any other prescribed course of treatment. I would continue seeing my counselor and take God's Word as my stabilizing prescription. Little did I know at the time that my journey into the life I always wanted had just begun. I was stepping into the path of freedom and had no idea how it would forever change me.

A New Relationship with God's Word

I learned something vital about God's Word during this time. First off, I finally recognized that all Scripture was meant for me. It was personally relevant and had direction for my life. In 2 Timothy 3:16 we read that "all Scripture is God-breathed and is useful for teaching, rebuking, correcting, and training in righteousness, so that the [woman] of God may be thoroughly equipped for every good work."

God's Word was given to us for our practical, everyday lives. It was meant to be our support, our foundation, the very instruction that would light our path to freedom. God's Word tells us what will work for us and what won't work for us. It teaches us, trains us, and equips us. God's Word became a letter to my soul, a voice from heaven, and a balm for my hurting heart. Rather than cramming myself with information to teach a Bible study, I was taking it in, listening to God speak to me, and for the very first time I was experiencing true life transformation. Unfortunately, for many years I had been reading God's Word like it was a speed-reading assignment, or something to be checked off my to-do list. Now was the time to soak in it and let it penetrate me. I had no idea that staying with one portion of Scripture day after day could be so life changing.

> For the word of God is living and active. Sharper than any double-edged sword, it penetrates even to dividing soul and spirit, joints and marrow; it judges the thoughts and attitudes of the heart.
>
> Hebrews 4:12

As I began to realize the value of meditating on one or two passages at a time, I likened it to soaking in the truth. Think of what it is like to marinate something. For example, imagine putting a bland boneless chicken breast in some teriyaki marinade for the day. When you come home, that chicken is a new color, a new texture, and a new flavor. When we marinate, or soak, in God's truth, something different takes place in us: we are changed from the inside out. Our attitudes, our hearts, and our mind-sets change. And for me, even the nasty depression I was seeped in slowly began to lift when my mind was drenched in simple repeated truths on a daily basis. My perspective was changing, and I was becoming a new woman. No more speed reading for me—this was a whole new way of relating to God. I was stripped bare and back to basics.

I didn't do this for just a week or a month. I read Psalm 139—morning, noon, and night—every day for just about a year. If the Word was going to be my medication, I would have to take it regularly. Like any other prescription I was required to take it in regular doses. At about the three-week mark, I started actually feeling different. I was stabilizing emotionally. Hope was starting to stir within me, and I was even daring to think that God himself might not be mad at me but that he might really be in love with me. Slowly I began to tackle some of those stuck spots that my counselor had so patiently waited for me to look at.

Most people who are suffering from a chemical imbalance benefit from prescribed medication. If you are in the pit of depression you may benefit from medical intervention. But a doctor will tell you that the medical balance is only half of the equation. The chemical balance is important because it enables us to deal with life and the processing of whatever circumstance or pain we are in. But the medicine cannot change our circumstances, our choices, our perspectives, or the things we have believed for years. We, as we are becoming balanced, must choose to deal with those. There are many Christian counselors who have committed their lives to helping Christians process through pain in a safe, constructive, and biblically balanced way. As believers we need to make sure that our process of dealing with false beliefs is based solely on the truth of God's Word. Remember—truth sets us free—his Word heals us in ways a medicine cannot. The right medication can retain balance; processing with a counselor, pastor, or safe person can help us sort through the messes of life; and the Word of truth can produce freedom and open our spiritual eyes that we might truly be healed. But we must be sure that we don't omit the most important thing in our journey to healing and freedom—the Word of God. Truth sets us free.

While soaking in the words of Psalm 139 I began to see four truths.

- He knows me.
- He protects me.
- He made me.
- He values me.

I had read this psalm before and never saw what I was seeing this time. Now these very obvious truths popped out at me. These truths gave me something to hang on to, something to sink my teeth into. So I repeated these truths over and over, I said them out loud, I prayed them, I wrote them on index cards and carried them around with me, and I began to ask God to show me what he was trying to say to me.

Slowly I began to believe the truth of God's involvement in my life and his love for me as I never understood it before. My prayers became frequent little conversations and affirmations of his love throughout my day.

"Lord, I thank you that you know me, you 'get me' and all my hurt, all my past, all my pain. I ask you to have your way in me because you know me better than I know myself."

A Changed Belief System

Call me crazy, but something happened to me. And, it's the deepening of faith, the changing of my life, and the healing of my soul. It's been over thirteen years since the depression lifted, and my life has changed. Knowing the reality of God's love for me now fuels me with a passion to share with other women—women like myself who need these same healing truths.

It's not what we know, it's what we choose to believe and live out that changes things. We live based on what we really believe, and our choices are based on the core belief system that we live by. Through disciplined focus on God's Word, my belief system changed. The negative perceptions of my childhood and past were replaced by the truth of God's love for me as his own. You can have knowledge, but it's action and belief in that knowledge that will take you to the next step. Do you want to go to the next step? I do.

I used to work in an industry where I trained the employees and weight-loss counselors for a large weight-loss organization. In that position I knew the calorie count, exchange amount, and the tools that someone needs to lose unwanted pounds. I gave classes, worked with individuals, and helped weight-loss counselors learn to set up individualized programs for their clients. I was a walking, talking caloric resource. During this time I gained twenty-five pounds! Go figure.

I knew all the information in my head but didn't live it out in my own life. I was depressed and turning to food and doing just the opposite of what I was telling others. I felt conflicted with my own weight spiraling out of control and decided to start looking for another job—and during that time I gained another ten pounds!

Looking back I now realize that this is a classic example of how it's not what you know that makes a difference, it's the choices you make based on what you know and believe. In the spiritual equation we can know all the verses by memory, but if we haven't accepted them as truth to apply to our own lives, we will remain stuck with a lot of head information with little life transformation. All the calorie counts, gadgets, and articles in the world did not keep me from gaining weight. Why? Because I didn't apply a single one of them to my own life.

Heart transformation takes place when we begin to take steps to act on the truth that we are learning. When Christ is found in the words of Scripture and those words become living bread for our souls, things change. And when we take a step to apply those words to our daily worlds, things really change.

I have found over and over again that we as women need to go back to basics. The words that we have come to think of as clichés are actually the life-changing classic truths. Instead of discounting them, it's time to learn how to live in them—for some this will be a new kind of Christian life.

Brennan Manning in *Abba's Child* writes,

> God created us for union with Himself: This is the original purpose of our lives. And God is defined as love (1 John 4:16). Living in awareness of our belovedness is the axis around which the Christian life revolves. Being the beloved is our identity, the core of our existence. It is not merely a lofty thought, an inspiring idea, or one name among many. It is the name by which God knows us and the way He relates to us.[2]

Understanding His Love

In order to be in union with God, we must understand what his love means to us personally. The truths of Scripture are meant to be lived. In order to be lived, truth must first be planted deep into our hearts. First Corinthians 13 is often known as the "love chapter." We hear it read at weddings, and we usually take the chapter and make a list of how we are to love other people. But before loving others in this way we must understand that God himself is love (1 John 4), and because he has defined himself as such, the characteristics of love as outlined in 1 Corinthians 13 apply to God's relationship with us. Let's put on new eyes and look at it as a declaration of God's relationship to us.

God's love suffers long and is kind toward me.

God's love does not envy.

God's love does not parade itself, is not puffed up.

God's love does not behave rudely.

God's love does not seek its own.

God's love is not easily provoked.

God's love thinks no evil but believes the best in me.

God's love does not rejoice in sin, and forgives the sinner.

God's love rejoices in the truth and covers me with grace.

God's love bears all things, believes all things, endures all things.

God's love never fails. His love is steadfast—fixed, firm, and unchanging.

Remember that 1 John 4:16 says "God is love." This is the nature of who God is. This is the good news. He is patient with us, he bears with us in our stupid choices, his love will never fail us. It isn't God who is telling us we are not enough and who is keeping us at arm's length. It isn't God who is discouraging us by holding up measuring sticks that represent a woman we can never be. No, it's not the love of God that is holding us down and keeping us back. Now is the time to believe, making truth our reality. As I continued soaking in the truth, my perspective was changing, my heart was changing—my life was changing.

Now add to 1 Corinthians 13 some basic truths pulled out of Psalm 139:

1. God knows me; I am not a stranger to him.
2. He understands me as an individual.
3. He is intimately acquainted with me.
4. He knows me well enough to know what I'll say next.
5. He is covering me; I am protected.
6. He is always with me.
7. I cannot separate myself from the love of God.
8. He leads me.
9. He holds my hand.
10. My life is not in darkness but basks in his light.
11. He made me, putting all the pieces together.
12. I am a wonderful work of God's hand.
13. My life is a miracle.
14. My days have been ordained (planned and purposed) by God.
15. His thoughts are tender toward me.
16. He is always thinking of me.
17. God preserves me from day to day.
18. When I wake to start a new day, he is still with me.
19. I am alive this moment by his design and plan.

Remember: Jesus said, "You will know the truth, and the truth will set you free" (John 8:32). He desires truth in our inward parts. He longs for us to know him and his love for us. It is this love that continues to call us.

Can you hear him calling? He is saying, "Come . . ."

Come back to the basic essential truths that can set you free.

Come back to the place of my love for you.

Come back to worshiping me in spirit and in truth.

Come, my daughter, I have something more than you have experienced before.

Start today by believing my words, one verse at a time.

For Further Reflection

1. Read all of Psalm 139. What kind of relationship with God is portrayed through David in this psalm?
2. How many things on the "life happens" list have you had at any one time? What do you do when you are stressed out?
3. Read Matthew 7:24–27. Given that foundation is important, what is the condition of your life's foundation at this moment?
4. In your daily life, are you generally more conformed to the pattern of this world or transformed by the truth of God's Word? How could you make changes that would affect which way your life and actions sway?
5. In Hebrews 4:12, God's Word is likened to a spiritual knife. That being truth, what in your life needs to go under the Great Physician's knife? How would spiritual surgery, or a faith lift, change your life?

6

God Knows Me

i Can Learn to Relax and Let Go

You have a God who hears you, the power of love behind you, the Holy Spirit within you, and all of heaven ahead of you.

Bob Coy

The most tender expression of God to me is simply that he knows me. I had never fully realized the impact of what it meant to be loved by someone who knew me so thoroughly. As I mined the truths in Psalm 139, God was taking my old beliefs and replacing them with new ones. Let's look at this first truth together.

He Knows Me

O LORD, you have searched me and you know me. You know when I sit and when I rise; you perceive my thoughts from afar. You discern my going out and my lying down; you are familiar with all of my ways. Before a word is on my tongue you know it completely, O LORD.

In Psalm 139:1–4, it says that God, the Creator of all things, knows me—he gets me, he understands my weaknesses, he knows my past hurts and painful thoughts. Yes, he knows me.

This was great news for someone who was getting tired of telling her own story!

I tried several counselors, and with each new appointment I had to start from the beginning. I realized one day during the course of reading the psalm that God already knew me completely, and he was able, ready, and willing to heal my heart. I continued to work with a counselor, and God used the truth of being known to give me the courage to be completely honest and continue toward healing.

The word *know* is from the Hebrew *yada*, which means he is personally acquainted with you, he knows you by experience, he knows you completely. It's personal knowledge derived from participation and observation.

How can you personalize this? What is this saying to you?

- He knows your every move.
- He knows your thoughts.
- He knows your idiosyncrasies.
- He is familiar with all you do and all you've done.
- He knows your insecurities.

- He knows your moods and attitudes.
- He knows what you will say next.
- He knows the condition of your heart (out of the heart the mouth speaks, and he knows what you will say before you say it!).
- He knows the past, present, and future.

As we will see later, he has been with you every single moment of your life. That means he's familiar with you. He's informed about you. This is good news if you are anything like me and trying to figure yourself or your life out.

I can remember what a relief it was to realize that God knows me. When I began to embrace the truth that he knows me, I began to have hope that, since he has been there in every detail of my life, he knows what makes me tick. And if he "gets me" then he can heal me more effectively than anything or anyone else. Hope began to put down roots.

This opened a whole new understanding to me. I began to realize that God knew my buttons, knew my vulnerabilities, knew my dreams and heart longings, and knew exactly where he was ultimately taking me in life. I just had to learn to embrace this very comforting truth . . . he knows me.

Psalm 139 says that God perceives our thoughts and that before a word is on our tongue he knows it completely. Amazing. He knows our thoughts and knows what we are going to say before we say it. Matthew tells us that Jesus knew the thoughts of the Pharisees and addressed them according to their thoughts, not according to what they were doing. Jesus also said in Matthew 12:34 that out of the overflow of the heart the mouth speaks. So if what I say comes from the depths or overflow of what is stuffed in my heart, and if the God who knows me is aware of what I will say next, then this same God is not shocked by what is in the deepest part of me, because he knows it already.

He is not shocked but instead compassionately coming after me that I might receive a new heart, one that is moved to follow in his ways. We must always remember that the heart is very important to God.

> Man looks at the outward appearance, but the LORD looks at the heart.
>
> 1 Samuel 16:7

> Above all else, guard your heart, for it is the wellspring of life.
>
> Proverbs 4:23

> A man's heart reflects the man.
>
> Proverbs 27:19

So if God knows me enough to know what I am thinking and what I will say, he certainly knows my heart—its condition, its hurts, its pains, and its dysfunction. And this was by far some of the best news I had ever heard. Now, instead of hiding in shame from God, I was becoming free to express myself to him, knowing there was nothing I could hide anyway. This was the true beginning of my healing—to realize that the God who knows me was inviting me to come to him and move away from my lame hiding.

Many of us have believed the wrong things about ourselves. We have taken in lies for so many years that we don't know how to internalize truth. Truth is foreign to us and sometimes a bit unbelievable. So we hide. Remember, we don't hide in bushes like Adam and Eve did, but we hide in performance and perfection. We hide behind the perfect body or within an imperfect one. We hide in relationships, in success, and in associations. We hide behind smiles and nice words. Somehow we seem to trick ourselves into thinking that it's possible to hide from God—but it's not.

> I know where you stay and when you come and go and how you rage against me.
>
> 2 Kings 19:27

> Does he not see my ways and count my every step?
>
> Job 31:4

> If we had forgotten the name of our God or spread out our hands to a foreign God, would not God have discovered it, since he knows the secrets of the heart?
>
> Psalm 44:20–21

> Your heavenly Father knows what you need.
>
> Matthew 6:8

The God Who Understands

God knows you better than you know yourself and has reached his verdict: he loves you still. No discovery will disillusion him; he loves you with an everlasting love. The God of the universe is not only interested in us, but he "gets us." It's hard to grasp, but it's important to believe, because it's the truth.

I wish I could say I know all the answers, but I don't. Most of the time I don't even "get" me or know how to fix the parts of me that are broken. But finally I was beginning to see the value and beauty of connecting to God in an up-close-and-personal relationship. This is the God who was not only powerful on my behalf but committed to my very soul.

Remember Carly, the young, hurting woman I met at Vacation Bible School? God knew her. He knew what needed healing, and it was far deeper than her husband or his situation. It had everything to do with what was planted within her from a young age that had never been exposed to the light of God's truth.

Carly sought professional help and was diagnosed with double depression, which meant she had been suffering from depression for a very long time. Her new life circumstances just added another depression to an underlying chronic depression. She was able to take the medication her doctor prescribed and began her road to chemical and emotional balance. As she followed the doctor's orders and began seeing a counselor, she also threw herself into the Great Physician's care by learning to soak in the truth too. All of these things were part of her eventual healing.

Yes, God in his faithfulness *knew* Carly and was leading her to discover the woman that he had always created her to be—as free as a butterfly escaping the cocoon. She began to flit, fly, and soar. The first step for Carly was the same as it had been for me. She had to get real. The next step was that she had to get back to the basic truth of the Bible. As she acknowledged her depression and sought medical intervention, God was faithful to do the spiritual healing she needed.

Janice wasn't depressed but chronically insecure. Even though she was thirty-seven, she hadn't progressed emotionally since graduating from college. Her insecurities caused havoc in all her relationships. She didn't feel she was enough, and so she assumed that everyone else was assigning her that fate too. This made her defensive and hypersensitive and caused her to talk others down to build herself up.

You might wonder . . . how can this be if Janice is a Christian? Doesn't she know that she is accepted in Christ? Well, most of us as Christian women could use a reality check with God's Word. It would do wonders for us in helping us lay down our immature insecurities. It all goes back to what is true and what is not. If we knew the truth and learned to lean into it, we would not be so apt to compete, compare, and compromise who we were called to be as his.

We need to make friends with the truth—God's truth! When we do, that perfect love changes us. Let's take a closer look at this powerful truth found in Psalm 139 (verses 1–4). I have included some different versions; maybe you can try reading them out loud.

> LORD, you have examined me and know all about me. You know when I sit down and when I get up. You know my thoughts before I think them. You know where I go and where I lie down. You know everything I do. LORD, even before I say a word, you already know it.
>
> NCV

> O LORD, you have examined my heart and know everything about me. You know when I sit down or stand up. You know my every thought when far away. You chart the path ahead of me and tell me where to stop and rest. Every moment you know where I am. You know what I am going to say even before I say it, LORD.
>
> NLT

> God, investigate my life; get all the facts firsthand. I'm an open book to you; even from a distance, you know what I'm thinking. You know when I leave and when I get back; I'm never out of

your sight. You know everything I'm going to say before I start the first sentence.

Message

David acknowledged that God knows everything. Because of this, God not only knew David's sins but also could forgive him. David turned his face to the altar of God. His heart yearned, as ours do today, for a personal, vital intimacy with God. He was seeking a new, real experience with his creator. Most of us know about God, but that is quite different from really knowing God. Our spiritual problems can only be solved by the God who created us. Isn't it logical to think that the only one who can re-create us is the one who created us in the first place? Part of starting over is embracing this truth.

To embrace: to clasp with the arms, to hug, to take up willingly.

So to embrace God's truth, think of wrapping your mind around it, hugging it with your heart, listening to it willingly and thoughtfully. The following verses of biblical truth may help you get your arms around the truth that he knows you.

His eyes are on the ways of men; he sees their every step.

Job 34:21

My eyes are on all their ways; they are not hidden from me.

Jeremiah 16:17

For the LORD watches over the way of the righteous.

Psalm 1:6

For all my ways are known to you.

Psalm 119:168

104

The LORD will fulfill his purpose for me.

Psalm 138:8

The Lord looks deep inside people and searches through their thoughts.

Proverbs 20:27 NCV

The Lord knows what is in everyone's mind. He understands everything you think. If you go to him for help, you will get an answer.

1 Chronicles 28:9 NCV

Hugging the Truth

Carly had to learn to hug truth too. Her new situation brought up past hurts that needed healing. She had grown up in a family where she learned to walk on eggshells with a father who alternated between rage and neglect and a mother who had been overwhelmed since Carly's premature birth. For many years she had hid secrets and shame that resulted in an eating disorder and was displayed in a body image problem. To others, she might have looked cute on the outside, but all that slender, pretty Carly could see was a fat, ugly, stupid, and never "good enough" girl.

God knew those hurts, and they all came to the surface when her husband became attracted to images of other women. Feelings of worthlessness ravaged her. But God knew her. He knew what needed healing. It had everything to do with all her beliefs, which were based on negative perceptions of herself, that had never been exposed to the light of God's truth. Yes, God in his faithfulness *knew* Carly and was leading her down a painful road, but the ultimate destination was the healing of her soul. Her crisis became her crossroads to a rich and intimate relationship with her Maker.

What part of you needs healing today? Have you been hiding yourself in shame from a God who already knows the details of your journey? Has your past prevented you from pushing on positively for a better future? Are you surprised to see that God knows you so well that he knows your thoughts, your heart's secrets, and even what will pop out of your mouth next? And that he still loves you despite all that?

I have received a lot of help from counselors, and I would not disregard how God has used good counsel in my life. But I couldn't depend on a counselor to fix me—I had to go to God with my heart and my hurts. I had to go to God with my mixed-up identity and my lack of self-worth. I desperately needed heart change, mind renewal, and the true miracle that could only come from truth setting me free. I needed faith to develop in the deepest part of me. Maybe you need faith to develop within you too. It starts with hearing the truth—and then hugging the truth.

Sometimes we aren't ready for the truth. We shield ourselves from truth, preferring to stay with the perceptions we have held on to for years. This is the case of a woman I met at a retreat—Dani. She certainly had bad programming, due to being raised by parents who verbally and physically abused her. She desperately wanted to believe good things about herself and her life, but she felt she couldn't.

I tried to tell her the truth, but she always countered with, "No, you don't understand, that's true of you but not of me." I finally had to get firm with her. Satan certainly had her in a stronghold of lies. She believed that what her parents did to her was who she was. As I tried to explain to her that she wasn't the abuse but she was a new woman in Christ, she kept coming up with excuse after excuse not to believe what the Word of God was clearly stating. It seemed obvious to me, but I began to realize that the pain she knew was more comfortable than the pain she didn't know. For her, it was frightening to believe the truth that she belonged to God and that he had been with her even in her earlier pain.

Though she had been a Christian for years she was bound up in the lies that her circumstances had imbedded into her soul. It was time for the freedom bell to ring for Dani! And that bell rang loud and clear as she began to take truth in one bite, one dose at a time, several times a day. She began the serious work of reprogramming her mind with truth, repeating it, thanking God for it, and acting on it. The process couldn't be rushed; it was like any other healing. And healing takes time.

Now take this first truth . . . *he knows me* . . . and begin thanking God for it. Let it run over and over in your mind. Write it out on a card or a sticky note or program it in your cell phone this week. Sit with it. Ask God questions about it. Let the truth that he knows you begin to take root. Hug the verse that hit you the most when you read it. Allow your thoughts, and eventually your heart, to connect with the truth. Stick with it. We are on a journey of understanding truth, daring to embrace it, and learning to believe it. It only takes the faith of a mustard seed. So nurture that little seed and get ready for God to do the miracle. And your history? Give that a hug too. There is not one part of your story that has been out of God's sight. Each and every circumstance will be used in some way by the God who was with you in each and every moment.

Remember—your history is his story in your life.

Personal Time Line

I have found it helpful to make a time line of my life, recalling snapshots of different events. Some pictures are positive and others negative. Some are neutral in emotion and some surprise me with the amount of emotional pain they stir up.

It's not a good idea to use your past as a gauge of your future. You are a new person in Christ. And it is not spiritually healthy to mull over your past, becoming obsessed with its pain. It is what it is. We cannot change our past, but we can use it as a rearview mirror, looking into it for clarity so we can move ahead safely and prevent ourselves from crashing into the same walls over and over again.

You may want to make a time line of your life. Start with the obvious—birth, special dates, and milestones. Then fill in with the snapshots of memory as God brings things to your mind; these snapshots can be as detailed or as vague as you want them to be. You may be surprised to find that there are moments of pain or change that you had forgotten about. Here is where it's important to hug the truth—God knows your history, and nothing is a surprise to him.

After outlining your history, go through and make notes of how God may have used the circumstances to eventually advance you closer to him. Remember—your history is his story in your life. And don't spend too much time in the rearview mirror. Just glance back, so you can get real with God about some of your pain and then allow him the opportunity to move you forward as you come to him.

Can you hear him calling? He is saying, "Come . . ."

Come to me with all your memories.
Come to me with all your joys, triumphs, pain, and sorrows.

Come to me because I know you, I am acquainted with every part of your story.

Come to me for I know my design, plan, and intent for your individual life.

For Further Reflection

1. Read Psalm 139:1–4. What stands out to you the most?
2. Given that "knows" means that God is personally acquainted with you, if you believed this at core level, what would change in your thinking and perspective?
3. What in your history are you not certain that God understands?
4. When looking in the rearview mirror of your life, what do you find the most troubling?
5. First Peter 5:7 says we are to cast our cares upon the God who cares for us. Is this easier to do when you understand that he not only cares but actually knows you better than you know yourself? How can you process the truth of God knowing you this well?

7

God Protects Me

i Can Have Faith instead of Fear

> I will protect him, for he acknowledges my name.
>
> Psalm 91:14

It's easy to feel all alone, unprotected, and vulnerable. There are many things in this life that can quickly stir up the emotion of fear. This fear tempts us to believe we are alone. But the truth tells us that we are not alone. The key is seeing the truth of God's presence in our life—even in our pain.

For years, I thought God's blessing and presence came when my performance was good enough or my circumstances were perfect enough. It was something new for me to see God as protector and keeper of my welfare in the times that were imperfect, sin stained, and messy.

So I could relate to Charlene when I met her. As this young single woman poured out her deep feelings of shame it was easy to see that due to her circumstances she had lots of questions concerning God's love for her. She is the first woman I've met who literally said to me, "Jesus loves me? So what." She had a hard time believing that Jesus could have allowed her to be unprotected from date rape, a circumstance that now kept her from pursuing any deep relationship with a man.

"Where was God, Debbie? Where was God when I trusted one of my best friends, and he violated me?" she asked. It was obvious that she was clearly bitter toward God for a circumstance that she had come to attribute to God rather than the person who had actually hurt and betrayed her.

Blaming God is common to us all. When life goes upside down, when bad things happen to us, it's easy to think, *If you are God and you are faithful and loving, where were you?* We forget that we live in a fallen world with fallen people. We live in a world where bad things happen.

Now through my meditation on the truth, God was challenging me to put my own questions aside once and for all and begin focusing on the truth that God indeed protects me. Painful circumstances still happen, but in the middle of the pain God takes what was meant for evil and turns it to good. God uses pain to have a purpose in my life.

If you have had similar questions and wrestlings about life circumstances, God is not shocked by your feelings. Remember the truth that he knows you, and in knowing you, he already knows the truth of what is in your heart. Despite what it looks like to you, God is protecting you, watching over you, and always mindful of you.

Charlene sat across from me with tear-stained cheeks and mouthed the words *I'm scared*. She went on to tell me that she was scared to let go of the fear and anger. If she let go and began believing God at this level, she would be out of control. Oh . . . did I understand what she was saying! I had a hard time with this particular truth too, but believing it ended up being the most freeing for me personally.

Release from Fear

I grew up with unreasonable fears. I am not exactly sure why I was so afraid, but I do know that my fears were so deep rooted that I didn't even take a shower during my growing-up years for fear that the noise would prevent me from hearing someone trying to come in and get me. And I hadn't even seen the movie *Psycho*. If I had seen that movie, my parents would have had to lock me up! Fear was part of my identity, though it definitely was a family secret. I looked confident on the outside, but within our walls it was no secret—Debbie was afraid of just about everything. As I grew up my fears only magnified, while the veneer I wore to hide the fears thickened. Fear in all forms is a very real emotion and a stealer of our joy and peace in Christ. Unfortunately many of us live as if we do not even believe God—instead we believe the fear-driven thoughts that we have always known. I was about to learn that there is a better way to live.

Many years earlier when I was a new Christian, I had a taste of what it would be like to live believing in the truth of God's protection. The night I accepted Christ was the first inkling I had that my fears could be conquered. For that moment in time, all fears were gone. That night I did something monumental for me—I took a shower. Yes, that's right, a shower. My parents were sleeping, and I slipped into the bathroom at 11:00 p.m. and took my very first home shower. I was so happy that I began to sing the choruses that I had heard that night, my first night at a Christian church. I was oblivious to the fact that I was singing pretty loud.

When I opened the bathroom door, both of my parents were standing there just staring at me. Quickly I began to explain, "I accepted Christ! I don't have to be afraid anymore! He's watching over me, and my life is in his hands!" I was so genuinely excited that I felt I could burst. Both my parents thought I had really gone over the top, and they were right—I had. And within six months they came over the top with me—accepting Christ too.

I wish I could tell you that my freedom from fear lasted indefinitely, and that fear, worry, and anxiety never raised their ugly heads again. But that is not the truth. You might be wondering, what happened to that girl who sang in the shower? Well, over time my focus changed from Christ and his love and provision for me, to living my life out in the best Christian way I could. One by one, my old fears returned.

Though I was a Christian and growing in my faith in Christian beliefs and doctrine, I was afraid to be alone, afraid in my house in the day or night, and couldn't read the paper or watch the news. I was a Christian singing songs of freedom, and I was *not* free.

No Fear in Love

I can't count how many times a woman has told me that she doesn't need to work on believing in God's love because she already understands that God loves her. Trouble is, she is expressing this as she is also telling me how she can't trust God in this area or that area. If we really believe God loves us, then why do we have reservations about trusting him? I think we need to get real about needing a fresh infusion of truth. We need to understand who he is and who we are to him.

We know that God's Word says he is a God of love. But we prove through our constant worry that what we know in our heads hasn't become part of our hearts.

> There is no fear in love. But perfect love drives out fear, because fear has to do with punishment. The one who fears is not made perfect in love.
>
> 1 John 4:18

There is really no way to deny the truth here. I experience fear when I do not trust God's love for me. Maybe I don't understand it and assume because life circumstances have hurt me that God must not be protecting me—therefore not loving me. Whatever the reason for my fear, I must acknowledge that I don't "get it," and that I need to understand his love on more than an intellectual level—I need it in my heart and on an emotional level. I need to learn how to live in the truth and reality of God's love . . . and so do you.

Jesus himself spoke of living in fear being equivalent to living as an unbeliever or pagan. Ouch! This doesn't mean that we are bad girls when we fear, it just means that he desires to wrap truth around our hearts so that we can learn that we really are safe. And he wants us to be sure in our belief system, so like the apostle Paul we can say, "If God is for me, who can be against me?" *Well*, you might be thinking . . . *lots of people can be against me.* True, they can—but even truer is that God will be with you in each and every circumstance. Even when you don't feel him there—he is with you.

Sometimes we do think that God is against us in our adversity. Pastor Bob Coy says,

> The bottom line is that God is looking for avenues through which He can gain glory, but these avenues don't always have to come

through our successes. God often gains even greater glory from the platform of our adversity.... If any man lived who knew intimately this alternate avenue of shining, it was Paul. From shipwrecks to beatings to stonings, he lived a life of sacrifice and hardship through which God's glory was clearly displayed.[1]

Was Paul protected in the middle of the trials and pain? Was his life filtered by a God who had a greater picture in mind? Yes, and Paul was learning how to accept God's presence in each event of his life, and acknowledged what it meant to be in the hands of a protective shepherd when he said, "His grace is sufficient for me."

Always in His Hand

It's no wonder then that as I read Psalm 139 I was deeply affected by the next truth—*he protects me*. I began to realize that it was time to put away the childish measuring stick that uses circumstances to measure God's love for me. It was time to start believing the truth that God was surrounding me, even when I least felt like he was.

Here's truth:

> You hem me in—behind and before;
> 　you have laid your hand upon me.
> Such knowledge is too wonderful for me,
> 　too lofty for me to attain.
> Where can I go from your Spirit?
> 　Where can I flee from your presence?
> If I go up to the heavens, you are there;
> 　if I make my bed in the depths, you are there.
> If I rise on the wings of the dawn,

if I settle on the far side of the sea,
even there your hand will guide me,
your right hand will hold me fast.
If I say, "Surely the darkness will hide me
and the light become night around me,"
even the darkness will not be dark to you;
the night will shine like the day,
for darkness is as light to you.

Psalm 139:5–12

The word *hem* means to enclose or to shut in. In the King James Bible, the word used is *beset*, which can mean to confine. To confine is to keep within bounds or to place borders around. "Thou hast beset me behind and before, and laid thine hand upon me."

Let's think about what this means for our lives if we are going to take it in as truth. God, the master and creator of all things, the one who knows us and loves us, has enclosed us within borders that can only be penetrated if he allows. Our lives are filtered by God's protection and love for us. I have heard some people say that their lives are "Father filtered."

Look at these verses (note that each of these verses are the words of Christ):

No one can snatch them out of my hand.

John 10:28

You do not belong to the world, but I have chosen you out of the world.

John 15:19

Holy Father, protect them by the power of your name.

John 17:11

My prayer is not that you take them out of the world but that you protect them from the evil one.

John 17:15

I have told you these things, so that in me you may have peace. In this world you will have trouble. But take heart! I have overcome the world.

John 16:33

Our Lives Are Father Filtered

The other day as I made my normal morning brew of dark coffee, I took note of the filter. Each day I place a clean white filter in the coffeemaker before I put the ground coffee in. Then I add the water and turn on the heat. I am in complete control of this process. The water boils and trickles through the ground coffee, and what comes out in the pot is the brewed stuff. Nothing can get through the filter except the intended coffee.

The same is true for us. Our lives are in his hands, and he is the filter through which all things, good and bad, pass through. Heaven is perfect, and heaven's reality is our promise. But life here is not perfect; it's flawed. During the course of our days we will go through stuff. And what we go through will not be a secret to God. He will know, and he will protect us from the harm that Satan desires to cause us. He will actually use the very pages that we thought were the unprotected chapters of our lives to cause us to become different people than we would be without the sanctification of the pain. If a circumstance has passed through God's filter, then he will supply all we need in each circumstance.

Now, think of what verse 5 of Psalm 139 is saying: "The God of all creation, mighty in power, and able to save, hems you in behind, before, and then tops it off with his hand of blessing being upon you" (my paraphrase).

As I began reading and meditating on this verse, I had the mental picture of a box. My life was enclosed in a God box, and as I continued in the truths of Psalm 139 and learned to lean into his love for me, I began to realize that the God box was a safe place to be. Fear began losing its grip.

Maybe you are thinking, *That sounds nice, but if what you say is true, how do we answer the nagging "whys"? Why all the hardship? Why the bad diagnosis? Why the financial problems? Why the shattered dreams and broken heart? Why? Why? Why?*

Life is filled with questions. Remember, real life is littered with things like broken relationships, illness, grief, loss, crime, and sin. As believers we are not exempt from the world we live in. But as believers we can trust that in the midst of it all, we are being protected by the God who says he has overcome the world. Go to God in prayer with all your "whys." He can handle your questions, your hurts, and the real places of your heart. He wants us to know truth in the inward parts of us—because truth at this level will change us. A core truth to add to our belief system is that he protects us.

To protect: to guard from harm or to shield.

This doesn't mean that we will never face harm but instead that we will be shielded and will only face what God allows to cross the borders that he has placed around our lives. We will never have the answers to all of our whys, but we can learn to believe the truth that God is a faithful God who is loving and protecting.

> The LORD is my strength and my shield;
> my heart trusts in him, and I am helped.
>
> Psalm 28:7

The LORD is my rock, my fortress and my deliverer;
   my God is my rock, in whom I take refuge.
He is my shield and the horn of my salvation, my
   stronghold.

Psalm 18:2

It is hard for us to grasp that the Lord God really does enclose us, really does have a hem or border around us. Even David said, "Such knowledge is too wonderful for me, too lofty for me to attain." So he begins asking questions in response to that truth: "Where can I go from your Spirit? Where can I flee from your presence?" And no matter where we go, the truth is we are in the hollow of God's hand. This is exciting truth if we will dare to believe it.

Listen to what Jesus says in John 10:27–29 about his sheep—those who are his.

My sheep listen to my voice; I know them, and they follow me. I give them eternal life, and they shall never perish; no one can snatch them out of my hand. My Father, who has given them to me, is greater than all; no one can snatch them out of my Father's hand.

No one can snatch us out of the Father's hand!

Now look at what the apostle Paul tells us in Romans 8:31, 35, 37–39:

If God is for us, who can be against us? . . . Who shall separate us from the love of Christ? Shall trouble or hardship or persecution or famine or nakedness or danger or sword? . . . No, in all these things we are more than conquerors through him who loved us. For I am convinced that neither death nor life, neither angels nor demons, neither the present nor the future, nor any powers, neither height nor depth, nor anything else in all creation, will be able to separate us from the love of God that is in Christ Jesus our Lord.

Nothing can separate us from the love and protection of God! Nothing. Repeat that truth to yourself. Nothing can separate me from God's love and protection.

Linger for a moment with these verses from Psalm 23:1, 4–6:

The LORD is my shepherd, I shall not be in want. . . . Even though I walk through the valley of the shadow of death, I will fear no evil, for you are with me. . . . You prepare a table before me in the presence of my enemies. You anoint my head with oil; my cup overflows. Surely goodness and love will follow me all the days of my life.

God Is for Us

I began to see that though I was going through a very dark valley, one that felt very much like death, I could lean into this truth—*he protects me*—and I could learn to live in his love for me instead of fear. As I looked over the snapshots of my life I certainly could identify the many times God did cover me and protect me even though it didn't seem like it at the time. And I began to realize that everything was part of a much bigger picture—God's purpose and plan. And though none of us like to look at the book of Job because we all fear going through unpleasant times, discomfort, or suffering, I think we have missed a key point—that in the end God did prove faithful and that he was Job's protection through it all.

Look at how the story ended:

The LORD made him prosperous again and gave him twice as much as he had before. All his brothers and sisters and everyone who had known him before came and ate with him in his house. They comforted and consoled him over all the trouble the LORD had brought upon him, and each one gave him a piece of silver and a gold ring. The LORD blessed the latter part of Job's life more than the first.

Job 42:10–12

Bob Coy sums it up powerfully:

It begins to dawn on us that our lives are not really our own either. They belong to the almighty, all-knowing God who is the author of our dreams. Our knowledge of Him must be perfected if ever we are to trust in His ability to carry out our dreams and to do with our lives what is in our best interest. If we don't see Him as able, in control, and on our side, we will always be prone to second-guess what He's doing and try to take matters back into our own hands.[2]

As I continued to read Psalm 139 morning, noon, and night, more and more truth began to pop out in vivid colors that I had never known. Truth that I had taken for granted or paid little attention to was now remaking my internal world.

To help me keep this new focus I bought myself an inexpensive sports watch. I set the alarm to go off every hour on the hour. And each time it signaled its little *beep beep*, I turned it off and reminded myself of some truth out of Psalm 139. If I was alone I would thank God for the truth as I repeated it out loud, and if I was at work or around people, I would stop the beeping and silently thank God for the truth.

For example, noon might have found me with "Lord, I thank you that you protect me and that you have me enclosed in a safe place, and even though it sometimes feels out of control, you are in control." Then 1:00 p.m. might find me with "Thanks,

Lord, for being my protection. If you are for me, nothing can stand against me. In the end you will show yourself faithful on my behalf. I trust your protection." And 2:00 p.m. might find me repeating, "Lord, you are my protection, my shield, my shepherd, I will fear no evil, my life is in your hand, and nothing can separate me from your love."

You get the picture. By the time I had made it through the day, I was lining up my previously negative mental moments with truth and beginning to realize more and more freedom from fear.

> **Fear**: anxiety and agitation caused by the presence of danger, evil, or pain. It is dread, fright, or a feeling of uneasiness or concern. It's to be afraid of somebody or something, real or imagined. It is to expect with misgiving, to be uneasy or anxious about your life.

There are two ways to handle fears as they come up in our lives:

1. Destructively
2. Constructively

When handling my fears destructively I face all situations from a feelings-only base. It is in this place that my feelings lead me down the following path:

- Denial—I deny there's a problem.
- Defeat—once I realize there is one, I begin living as a helpless victim.
- Bitterness—I look around and blame someone else.
- Escape—I look for ways to run away from reality; after all, the grass might be greener somewhere else.

But when learning to handle my fears constructively, I begin to face my problems with a faith base rather than a feelings-only base. I acknowledge my feelings and learn to come to God with all the feelings and fears that are inside of me. In this place I might be led down the following path:

- Sorrow—I admit there's a problem and stop trying to fix it.
- Brokenness—I acknowledge the need for God's strength and power.
- Surrender—I say, "Father, save me!"
- Faith decision—I place all that concerns me into God's hands.

As I drank in the message of Psalm 139:5, I found relief. Reflecting on the truth that God goes before me, follows behind me, and places his hand on me gives me a picture of God enclosing me in his love. We cannot see the hands of God, but it is essential to believe by faith that his hands are always there upholding us, protecting us, and guiding us. Do you think that God is big enough to take care of the things that are holding you in the grip of fear?

Remember, chronic fear is a gauge for where we are in getting the message of God's love from head to heart. We have not matured in love while living in chronic fear. Or maybe we just forgot about the power and presence of that love and need to remind ourselves of the truth. It is a personal prayer of mine to understand the love of God in such a way that fear would not be a chronic heart/mind condition.

I realize there are times of "normal" fear, such as the apprehension when you see someone coming straight for your bumper through the rearview mirror, or when you walk into your house after a burglary, or when a doctor presents a bad diagnosis. We all experience real fear now and then. This is normal. It is these kinds of fears that cause us to use common sense, wear our seat belts, lock our doors, and get treatment for medical conditions.

The fear this verse talks about is the fear that torments and punishes you. The fear that things are not going to be okay with you. The kind of fear that says, "There is not a God of love watching over me." It is the kind of fear that has reduced God's love and protection to some fairy tale instead of the real strength and power that it is. It is the kind of fear that says, "God is for everyone else, but not me." Fearing the future, fearing the unknown, fearing illness, fearing disability, fearing rejection, fearing vulnerability, fearing growing old, fearing for our children, fearing for our friends, fearing that the worst you think about yourself is the absolute truth—fear, fear, fear. Lord, help us believe!

His call is getting clearer and clearer. He says, "Come . . ."

Come to me with all of your fears.

Come to me with your cares—remembering that I care for you.

Come to me and learn to take heart! Walk in courage!

For Further Reflection

1. Read Psalm 139:5–12. What speaks to you the most about God's covering over your life?
2. Does it help you to understand the God box around your life? What situations can you look back on and point to that enclosure of protection around you even though you were in a bad situation?

3. For all the times you felt unprotected, how does this passage of Scripture relate to you?

4. First John 4:18 says that fear is actually tormenting. Have you ever felt tormented or mentally punished by your fears? How can knowing God's love and involvement in your life be an antidote for fear?

5. What does handling fear destructively look like to you? In contrast, what would handling fear constructively look like?

8

God Made Me

i Am Significant Because He Says So

Long before any human being saw us, we are seen by God's loving eyes. Long before anyone heard us cry or laugh, we are heard by our God who is all ears for us. Long before any person spoke to us in this world, we are spoken to by the voice of eternal love.

Henri Nouwen

The next truth that I poured over my heart was—*he made me.* This truth out of Psalm 139 helped me acknowledge God's hand and plan in my birth and life. From my earliest memory I always felt I was defective in some way. To believe that my life was actually a miracle of God-sized proportions was hard to grasp—even harder to believe for more than a fleeting moment.

It's always been easy for me to be in awe of the miracle of life when I see the perfectly formed tiny fingers and toes of a new baby. But when it comes down to me, well, that's always been another story.

Let's take a look at the truth—*God made me.*

> For you created my inmost being;
>> you knit me together in my mother's womb.
> I praise you because I am fearfully and wonderfully
>> made;
>> your works are wonderful,
>> I know that full well.
> My frame was not hidden from you
>> when I was made in the secret place.
> When I was woven together in the depths of the earth,
>> your eyes saw my unformed body.
> All the days ordained for me
>> were written in your book
>> before one of them came to be.
>
> Psalm 139:13–16

He created me. This truth began to make sense to me for the very first time. He didn't just create the world, the moon, stars, trees, and oceans—he created *me.*

Like most women I *ooh* and *aah* over new life. I marvel at each intricate feature from head to toe because there is such promise and possibility associated with new life. A new life is fresh—like a clean slate, a new beginning. Once this little person enters the scene, nothing will ever be exactly as it was before.

So it is with us! At one time we were the little ones that people *oohed* and *aahed* over. They looked at all our features to determine just who we looked like, and they hoped in the promise of tomorrow. What about stopping right now to recognize the promise and miracle of your life . . .

Now sink your thoughts into the following verses:

So God created man in his own image, in the image of God he created him; male and female he created them . . . God saw all that he had made, and it was very good.

Genesis 1:27, 31

Your hands made me and formed me.

Psalm 119:73

Before I formed you in the womb I knew you, before you were born I set you apart.

Jeremiah 1:5

I have upheld you since [you] were conceived, and have carried [you] since your birth.

Isaiah 46:3

For it was in Him that all things were created, in heaven and on earth, things seen and things unseen, whether thrones, dominions, rulers, or authorities; all things were created and exist through Him (by His service, intervention) and in and for Him.

Colossians 1:16 Amplified

For we are God's workmanship, created in Christ Jesus to do good works, which God prepared in advance for us to do.

Ephesians 2:10

For in him we live and move and have our being. As some of your own poets have said, "We are his offspring."

Acts 17:28

Healing My Past

From the time I was a little girl I always suspected there was something wrong between my mother and me. Being we were both adult Christian women, I decided to ask her the hard question.

"Mom, I know there has always been something wrong, and I need to know what it is. I know there has always been something between you and me. I think that there must be something wrong with me, seeing as my own mother is so critical of me."

She turned her head toward the wall, and I could see a tear coming down her cheek. Then with the humblest expression she said to me, "I never wanted to tell you this. I am so ashamed."

She then went on to explain to me her life and her hurts from her earliest childhood loss of her own father to her unhappy marriage to my father. She had secretly planned to leave my father when my sister was twelve. Instead she ended up pregnant with me. Then she had a troubled pregnancy and ended up in bed the whole time. She didn't want me. Now, because of the baby in her womb, she couldn't leave my dad, and she resented me for it.

But as she was coming toward the end of the pregnancy she began to have warm thoughts about the coming baby. When I was born she had true love feelings for me, just as she had when her first child was born twelve years earlier. But I was a colicky baby, and I would often cry and be inconsolable in my mother's arms. But when she handed me over to my drunken father, I would quiet down like a happy little lamb.

When I was about six months old my mother made a decision. She decided that this child would never hurt her. And to make sure that happened she began to keep herself at arm's length from her little girl's heart. She provided all my material needs but would never allow herself to emotionally connect.

Now when I confronted her on this, she cried and said she was so sorry. She let me know how hard it was to watch me as I tried so hard to prove myself to her during my childhood. She admitted that she knew what I was doing, but in her stubbornness she couldn't let go and let me in. This explained a lot.

Together we began healing our relationship, though I must admit I don't think we ever had enough time. My own mother finally told me all the words I needed to hear. She even told me I was pretty for the very first time a few months before she died. As I lay in her hospital bed with her, she stroked my face, her eyes filled with tears, expressing again how sorry she was that she waited so long to let me know how she felt about me. She was seventy-eight, and I wanted her to live forever. But she died that summer. I will always love her, and I think of her every single day.

Three Needs

Most women struggle with believing they have significance. It is said that low self-esteem, which is having an unhealthy estimation of who we are, is the number one cause of depression in women. Self-esteem goes much deeper than the surface things like our looks; it begins and ends with the realization that our lives have purpose and value.

Though we are different, each of us has three specific needs in common:

1. The need to belong
2. The need to be unique
3. The need to be needed

These needs are met in understanding the awesome truth that God himself created us, and he created us as part of his overall story and plan. Each one of us has a part to play because God created us for his purposes. The truth *God made me* might sound simplistic, but it is very powerful when embraced. This truth settles the score, enabling us to get over ourselves so that we can learn to live, as Oswald Chambers says, being our utmost for his highest.

Because God is the creator and the signature of God is on our lives, we have value. Add to that the blood of Christ being shed for our redemption, and we can see we were important enough to die for. And then think of the Holy Spirit being deposited into us upon salvation and we have a clear picture of significance. Why would God make such provision for us if we had no value to him or his plan?

This understanding brings about a God-confidence that far outshines the flimsy confidence that we try to claim for ourselves through being pretty, perfect, and polished. This confidence is about our position as his. This confidence is about faith and not about our fleeting feelings. This confidence can change your life.

Created in the Image of God

Several years ago we had an African children's choir visit our church. They were darling children who danced and sang their way into the hearts of the people attending services that Sunday. During one of the songs they marched around the stage, smiling enthusiastically as they sang, "I am a promise. I am a possibility. I am a promise, with a capital P." Then they went into, "I am somebody, yes, I'm somebody. Created in the image of God, yes, I'm somebody."

I watched the adults in the church smile broadly back while nodding in agreement to the words of the song. And then I wondered . . . do we get this? Do we even understand our significance? Does each of us believe that we are an important part of the picture—created by the Almighty? Or have our insecurities and the prevalent lies of our culture robbed us of the worth that God himself has assigned to each of us? Does the cultural message that we have to do something valuable to be valuable change the way we view this powerful basic truth?

Scripture says that God himself created us for his own purpose. We also see that Scripture says God knit us together in our mother's womb. Imagine the God who created the universe, the author of creativity, weaving us together stitch by glorious stitch, all fashioned for his story, his plan, and his purposes.

In the KJV, the knitted in our mother's womb verse reads, "Thou hast possessed my reins." In the original Hebrew the word for possessed is *quanah*, which means to create or erect, to purchase, recover, redeem. The original Hebrew for the word *reins* is *kilyah*, which means an essential organ such as the mind (interior self) or the kidney. This word comes from the word *kliy*, which means something prepared, as in a vessel or utensil.

How amazing to think of the magnificent plan that was being accomplished in our mother's womb. He created us fully—our interior self, such as our mind, emotions, personalities, and our essential physical qualities. All was created as God himself was preparing a vessel for his use! A vessel that God plans to use for his purposes is certainly something or someone of significance!

This is a beautiful example of all of Scripture meeting and coming together. God the Father created us, and Jesus the Son (God in the flesh) came to recover us and redeem us from being born into a sinful world. We were born of our mother's womb, but Jesus said that we must also be born of the Spirit, and that is what he came to do—redeem us and restore us to his original design. Truth can enable us to define ourselves and look at ourselves differently.

> So from now on we regard no one [not even ourselves] from a worldly point of view. . . . Therefore, if anyone is in Christ, he [or she] is a new creation; the old has gone, the new has come! All this is from God, who reconciled us to himself through Christ and gave us the ministry of reconciliation. . . . We are therefore Christ's ambassadors, as though God were making his appeal through us. We implore you on Christ's behalf: Be reconciled to God.
>
> 2 Corinthians 5:16–18, 20

Take a look at these key words of this passage:

- **regard**—from the Greek meaning know, understand, or recognize
- **worldly point of view**—from the original Greek that would mean flesh, body, made of the flesh, human, sinful nature, unspiritual
- **in (Christ)**—with reference to, to be included or contained in
- **new creation**—from the original word meaning creature
- **gone**—past, dead, absorbed
- **come**—to move into view or position, to exist at a particular place or point
- **ambassadors**—highest rank of representative in residence to another
- **appeal**—from the original Greek word meaning call, urge, invite
- **reconciled**—to bring into acceptance, to reestablish friendship between, to settle all opposing views

When I put this into my own words and apply the meaning behind the key words to my life, it looks like this:

So from now on I am not to know, understand, or recognize myself from a worldly point of view. This view is unspiritual and just has to do with the flesh and body. Instead I am to reference myself as someone contained in Christ as a completely new being and person. The person I was before is now dead and has been absorbed through the death and life of Christ in me. The new me must move into view and become the position that I live, breathe, and stand in. Because of Christ I am a representative of God, as his Spirit has taken residence in me. I am to live not for myself but for Christ, making a call for Christ, urging others to be reestablished in relationship with him. I am to be settled in who I am as a new person in Christ, and am to stand firm against any opposing views of myself or others.

Eugene Peterson says it this way in the Message:

Our firm decision is to work from this focused center: One man died for everyone. That puts everyone in the same boat. He included everyone in his death so that everyone could also be included in his life, a resurrection life, a far better life than people ever lived on their own.

Because of this decision we don't evaluate people by what they have or how they look. We looked at the Messiah that way once and got it all wrong, as you know. We certainly don't look at him that way anymore. Now we look inside, and what we see is that anyone united with the Messiah gets a fresh start, is created new. The old life is gone; a new life burgeons! Look at it! All this comes from the God who settled the relationship between us and him, and then called us to settle our relationships with each other. God put the world square with himself through the Messiah, giving the world a fresh start by offering forgiveness of sins. God has given us the task of telling everyone what he is doing. We're Christ's representatives. God uses us to persuade men and women to drop their differences and enter into God's work of making things right between them. We're speaking for Christ himself now: Become friends with God; he's already a friend with you.

How? you ask. In Christ. God put the wrong on him who never did anything wrong, so we could be put right with God.

2 Corinthians 5:14–21

Butterfly Girl

It is so important that we line up with the truth that we are new—the old is gone. We might not feel like we are new, but it's a decision of faith to dare to believe that it's the truth about us.

I began to ask myself some basic questions. How come I never "got" this truth down deep in my heart? What was blocking it? How could I learn to live it out now? Every time I had heard the new creature in Christ verse, I had always associated it with the idea of a butterfly, and I think it became just another unreal thought to me. But I was clearly beginning to be set free by the truth of what it was implying. It really wasn't about being pretty, perfect, and polished—it was all about position.

During this time I went looking for a baby picture of myself. This was quite a feat, being as there were not many pictures of me as a baby or young child. But I found a few. The youngest one I could find was me at probably age three on a pony, pouting and looking very upset. I took that photo and put that sad little Debra Marie in a frame that said "bloom where you are planted." This picture served as a constant reminder that God was with me from my earliest beginnings. He knew me and loved me then, and he knows me and loves me now.

I wasn't always who I am now, but all along I had been becoming who I am. Each thing in my life had been shaping me, and now the God of all creation was calling me to draw close to him for the ultimate reshaping of my life. That sad little face spoke volumes to me of my need to go back to basics and learn how to live in them, so much so that they would become my air, my life, my new reality.

A few years into this new journey, I took another little Debra Marie picture and put her in my Bible as a bookmark right there in Psalm 139. And each day as I opened up to the psalm, I was reminded that from my very earliest beginnings, God was not only with me, he created me. He not only created me, he created a plan for me etched into the fabric of who I was.

The interesting thing about this truth is the understanding that God actually knit us together, formed each thing about us for his purposes. I have heard it said that God prepacked us to use as he has planned. I love that. Now add the next part of the passage: "All the days ordained for me were written in your book." Whoa, that is amazing.

When we look at our life snapshots through the lens of this truth, we see that God doesn't waste a thing. Everything we have gone through, when turned over to him in surrender, will be a tool that he will use to shape us and move us to his intended plan. He is so involved in our lives, whether we realize it or not, that the apostle Paul says he even determines where we live:

> He himself gives all men life and breath and everything else. From one man he made every nation of men, that they should inhabit the whole earth; and he determined the times set for them and the exact places where they should live. God did this so that men would seek him and perhaps reach out for him and find him, though he is not far from each one of us. "For in him we live and

move and have our being." As some of your own poets have said, "We are his offspring."

Acts 17:25–28

As I began to realize the truth that God made me, makes no mistakes, and therefore values that which he has made, I also began to see the connection between his creation and his sovereignty over my life. The truth that he has ordained my days used to sound too lofty and theological for me to bring down to my own level. Though the word *ordain* can mean to install as a priest, it actually has meaning that relates practically to me. I was soon to see that this powerful biblical truth is completely life changing and capable of giving us a faith infusion.

Ordain: to prescribe, to call the shots, to set forth by express design.

In the Amplified version, Psalm 139:16 reads:

Your eyes saw my unformed substance, and in Your book all of the days of my life were written before ever they took shape, when as yet there was none of them.

The New American Standard reads:

And in Your book they were all written, The days that were ordained for me, When as yet there was none of them.

In him we were also chosen, having been predestined according to the plan of him who works out everything in conformity with the purpose of his will.

Ephesians 1:11

138

This big and mighty God not only made us but he ordained—or had a design for—our life. And it is this same God who works everything to conform to his purpose and his will. Understanding that I am part of history, part of the picture, is thrilling to me.

As I am growing in an understanding of the sovereignty of God and how he is at work in ways we don't fully see or realize, I have been watching God connect the dots to many different things. I stand in awe of how involved he really is—this knowledge has gone straight to the depths of my heart and comforts me when I am sad, gives me courage when I am slipping, and gives me hope to face the next day.

He is calling me daily to come closer. And each day I hear that same word . . . "Come." Can you hear him too?

Come to me because I know the plans I have for you.

Come to me, you are not a mistake, you are mine.

Come to me because I created you for a specific purpose.

Come to me because I know the bigger picture and can lead you there.

For Further Reflection

1. Read Psalm 139:13–16. What is the most significant truth in this passage?
2. What is the truth about your life? Are you a mistake? Or a miracle?
3. What are the gifts or abilities that you can acknowledge you were born with by God's plan and design?

4. Have you struggled with thoughts of worthlessness? Would it stand to reason that God would make something of no value?

5. What word is used to describe God's work? In Acts 17:29, we are told that in him we live and move and have our being. What does this mean to you today?

9

God Values Me

i Am Treasured, Cherished, and Loved

He has had you in His master plan so that He could shine His light through you in a way that can be only shone through you. You will stand up and be the history maker that God has designed you to be—because of the Grace of God.

source unknown

One day I went across the street to the neighborhood park and sat on the edge of the sandbox. As I sat there in the warmth of the sun, I was thinking of Psalm 139:17–18: "How precious to me are your thoughts, O God! How vast is the sum of them! Were I to count them they would outnumber the grains of sand." Before I knew it, I was picking up a handful of sand with the thought that I would see if it was countable. Well, it couldn't be counted. When I realized that not even a handful of sand could be counted, I got the picture—God values what he has made.

Value: the worth of something.

Worth: the value of something measured by the esteem in which it is held; having value.

Unfortunately we live in a culture that has skewed our worth and has encouraged us to base our worth on what we do rather than who we are as individuals who have been designed and created by God. When we are raised within this skewed value system, we become stifled and are kept in bondage. But our value has nothing to do with the exterior world but everything to do with our position—the position we are held in—in Christ.

Position: the place occupied by a person or thing.

Rank or status: to set in a particular spot.

Let's look at our particular rank or our particular spot in God's picture.

Child of God

How great is the love the Father has lavished on us, that we should be called children of God!

1 John 3:1

This is how God showed his love among us: He sent his one and only Son into the world that we might live through him.

1 John 4:9

Chosen by God

You are a chosen people, a royal priesthood, a holy nation, a people belonging to God, that you may declare the praises of him who called you out of darkness into his wonderful light. . . . Now you are the people of God.

1 Peter 2:9–10

Created for God

For by him all things were created . . . all things were created by him and for him. He is before all things, and in him all things hold together.

Colossians 1:16–17

Robert McGee says in *The Search for Significance,*

An accurate understanding of God's truth is the first step toward discovering our significance and worth. Unfortunately, many of us have been exposed to inadequate teaching from both religious and secular sources concerning our self-worth. As a result we may have a distorted self-perception, and may be experiencing hopelessness rather than the rich and meaningful life God intends for us.[1]

The Old Testament speaks of the worth and value of God's people in the book of Deuteronomy:

For you are a people holy to the LORD your God. The LORD your God has chosen you out of all the peoples on the face of the earth to be his people, his treasured possession.

Deuteronomy 7:6

Jesus Christ speaks of our value in the Gospel of Matthew:

143

Look at the birds of the air; they do not sow or reap or store away in barns, and yet your heavenly Father feeds them. Are you not much more valuable than they?

Matthew 6:26

Are not two sparrows sold for a penny? Yet not one of them will fall to the ground apart from the will of your Father. And even the very hairs on your head are all numbered. So don't be afraid; you are worth more than many sparrows.

Matthew 10:29–31

Earlier in the book I wrote about what the word *treasure* means in the Deuteronomy verse. It has been this verse that has helped me beyond measure to regain the proper focus of my position in the Father's heart. The following verse in context with Deuteronomy 7:6 helps bring out the entire picture.

The LORD did not set his affection on you and choose you because you were more numerous than other peoples, for you were the fewest of all peoples. But it was because the LORD loved you and kept the oath he swore to your forefathers that he brought you out with a mighty hand and redeemed you from the land of slavery. . . . Know therefore that the LORD your God is God; he is the faithful God, keeping his covenant of love to a thousand generations of those who love him.

Deuteronomy 7:6–9

Clearly we see that our worth and acceptability are not based on us. These things rest on God's love for those he created. He didn't choose us because we are the best pick for the team, the prettiest, the smartest, or the most talented. He chose us because he loves us.

Trouble is, we are accustomed to having to do something to earn the love of another. In this case, it's a free gift. This is why God's love is so hard to embrace and grasp. It's unnatural to our human reasoning.

The word *possession* here in the Hebrew is the word *cegullah*,[2] which signifies "property" in the special sense of a private possession that one personally acquired and carefully maintains or preserves. What a beautiful picture of who we are to Christ and in Christ. He personally acquired us: "While we were still sinners, Christ died for us" (Rom. 5:8). And then he even carefully maintains us. Jesus said, "No one can snatch them out of my hand" (John 10:28). Why? Because God declared us his personal treasure!

Jesus himself expressed our value when he told us we didn't have to worry—he knew our needs, even the number of hairs on our heads. He said we could have the freedom to live one day at a time. I once heard someone say, "Faith in God restores the missing sense of being somebody." Can you put your faith in the truth that you are his possession and his personal treasure?

> **Treasure**: accumulated or acquired wealth, one regarded as valuable, to cherish, to value greatly.

"His treasure" is what the Lord God calls us. We are his wealth. We are cherished and valued.

A biblical concept of self-worth goes beyond the limited goal of feeling good about ourselves. Instead of being based on feelings, a biblical view of self is an accurate perception of the truth about ourselves, God, and others based on what is found in God's Word. A biblical self-concept is a mix of both strength and humility, both sorrow over our sin and joy over grace and forgiveness, and a deep sense of our need for God's power, grace, and love.

There are many verses that shout the love of God for his people. But before I could even begin to drink in the sweetness of his love, I had to know that no matter what had happened in my life or how I felt, I still belonged to God. I had to tell myself the truth, and in so doing quiet the misbeliefs that I had held on to for so many years.

In the book *Telling Yourself the Truth*, William Backus and Marie Chapian write,

> Don't let anybody tell you that what you think or tell yourself isn't important. It was the main core of Jesus's teachings . . . it is a fact that has long been known to wise men, including the authors of Scriptures: Change a man's beliefs and you will change his feelings and behaviour. In order to accomplish this we must replace truth where there are misbeliefs in our lives.[3]

They go on to say, "The words we tell ourselves are more important than we realize. If you tell yourself something enough times and in the right circumstances, you will believe those words whether true or not."[4]

This passage generated some questions for me. Could I replace my old beliefs with truth?

I have been chosen by God?

I am his treasure? His possession?

He loves me, even me?

Could he finally deliver me from the slavery of self and non-authentic living?

Think of it . . . he calls us a treasure, his woman of worth.

I often personalize Scripture to make it my own. And in so doing, this verse (Deut. 7:6) speaks to my heart . . .

Debbie, you are a woman who is holy to the Lord your God, and he has chosen you, yes, you, out of all the people on the face of the earth to be his . . . his treasure, his property, the woman he carefully preserves through the ups and downs of life, the woman he is forming into all that he has planned for you to be . . . his possession.

You Are His Treasure

I have a curio cabinet filled with Boyd's bear figurines. Though they are relatively inexpensive, they are collectables and my little treasures. They are whimsical and make me smile. It's interesting what I do with these little bears . . . I display them, I protect them, I shine a light on them, and I know exactly where each one is placed within the cabinet—and why.

And these are just silly little bears!

When God calls us his treasure, it's another expression of identifying us as belonging to someone other than ourself. It is this belonging that gives us value. It is this belonging that can change the way we view everyone and everything. A healthy estimation of our self and our value—to be biblically correct—will always point back to God and his hand in creating us, and to Jesus and his blood that saved us from who we are apart from the Spirit of God living within us. It's up to us to accept that our worth is dependent on God's truth and not on the things we are used to relating it to.

Unfortunately, many of us are stuck in an unhealthy equation of:

$$\text{Self-worth} = \text{Performance} + \text{Others' Opinions}^5$$

This was the trap that kept me performing for many years. I didn't realize I was performing, but I was. I was constantly trying to do the right thing, the good thing, the best thing—so that others would be pleased with me and have a good opinion of me. I even deceived myself by thinking I was doing my best for God, even though much of it was really all about me and what I could do.

When my life crashed, I didn't have the energy to perform anymore. This was the best possible place for me to be—empty. Ready for God to do his work. God heard my prayers. He came after me with his love. Coming after people and answering prayer is the amazing work of the Father.

Coming after Elvis

Several years ago I was in Las Vegas for a trade show. I really don't care for Vegas and must admit to having a bit of an attitude. After one particularly long day, I was tired and asked to be excused from the party we were to attend that night. But in the line of duty, I had to attend. Too much had gone into the planning to just blow it off. So with a bad attitude, I went.

We were being taken by bus to the outskirts of town, to a mystery spot. There I was . . . grumpy me, trying to mingle with computer guys and instead being totally bored. I think the mystery of the evening was the three impersonators that they had entertaining us—Robin Williams, James Brown, and Elvis. For some reason Elvis kept trying to mingle with me throughout the night. I got the feeling he was a bit bored himself. In my grumpy state I found him completely annoying. I just wanted to be done with the party and get back to my hotel room. But I was stuck there, having to wait for the buses to come back for us at midnight.

So about an hour before the clock struck twelve, I got a folding chair and waited near the glass doors. I was going to be the first on the bus! When the buses came, I quickly boarded the one back to the Las Vegas Hilton. I picked a seat in the back so no one would bother me. I strategically placed my little bag of goodies and gifts on the seat next to me, making it completely unavailable. Closing my eyes, I was finally content in knowing I would soon be back in my room, curled up in bed, and away from a very long day and night.

The bus engine began to warm up, and we were ready to roll. But then the hydraulic sound of the bus door opening stopped us from leaving. I quickly thought to myself, *Oh no, please don't let it be Elvis!*

The bus driver let one last passenger in . . . and it was Elvis.

I looked up and upon seeing him thought, *Certainly he won't come to the back of the bus.* But to my horror, he began walking down the bus aisle straight toward my seat. And boy did I ever have a bad attitude when he came to the edge of my row and said in his Elvis persona, "Ma'am, is anyone sitting there?"

At once the Holy Spirit snapped my thoughts to attention with two words that shot through my heart: *be open.*

My mind began to race. *Be open? How does one be open to an Elvis impersonator?* Quickly I moved my stuff from my extra seat; my first act of being open was letting him sit there.

My mind was spinning. *Lord, how do I be open to him? What do I say?* All at once I began to say the dumbest thing, and as the words left my lips I felt ridiculous.

"Hey, are there ever any Elvis conventions in Las Vegas?"

Now out of persona, he answered, "No, but next year to commemorate the anniversary of Elvis's death there is going to be one."

In response to that I rattled off the date and year of Elvis's death, and that's when God started connecting those God ordained dots!

"You must be a big Elvis fan," he said to me.

"Nope, I was in a near fatal car accident the day that Elvis died. And while they were working on me in the emergency room, they thought I was unaware, but they kept talking about Elvis dying. I wanted to jump off the table and scream, 'Elvis is already dead, save me!' And since that was the day that God spared my life, I will never forget that day in August."

Suddenly our conversation dove to a spiritual depth that I never could have anticipated. Elvis introduced himself as Ernie, and he began telling me that he had been on a God-search for a whole year. He had tried all kinds of churches, listened to broadcasts, and asked God to show him if he was indeed real. And it all left him with one final prayer. He told me that he had been listening to some guy on the radio, but not totally trusting radio preachers, he asked God, "If this guy's for real and what he's saying is true, then I will have to meet someone who knows him." End of prayer.

As he told me this, I just knew in my heart that heaven's drum-roll was beginning!

"Well, Ernie, who's the preacher?"

"Oh, it's some cat from California, I think his name is Chuck. The show is 'Words for Today' or something like that."

"Do you think his name is Chuck Smith?"

"Yeah, that's it."

"Well, how about that. God brought a woman from the San Francisco area to Las Vegas, to a trade show she didn't want to attend, to a party that she just wanted to leave . . . all to answer your prayer, because God loves you and heard your call to him."

"Do you know this Chuck guy?"

"Yes, he was my pastor back in the seventies. Everything you hear on his radio broadcast is truth, straight from God's Word. Ernie, that's why you are sincerely drawn to it."

About this time the bus rolled up to the Las Vegas Hilton, and we began to exit. After getting off I looked up at Ernie, who had tears cutting through his stage makeup, and I said, "Are we done?"

He shook his head. "No . . ."

So there I was in Vegas at 12:30 in the morning with a guy crying in a white rhinestone outfit. I stood there quickly assessing the surroundings, wondering where to go and what to do.

I spotted a bench in front of the hotel, in clear view of all the passing people. Las Vegas at 12:30 a.m. is like 2:00 in the afternoon anywhere else . . . it was still action packed. And so we sat there on that public bench, and Ernie, realizing that God had answered his very specific prayer, gave his heart and life to Christ that night right there in front of the Las Vegas Hilton.

I could hardly wait to get back to my hotel room to call my husband. "Ray, Ray . . . I helped lead Elvis to the Lord!"

"Deb, have you been drinking?" (Quite a question, seeing as I am not a drinker!)

"No, it really happened, I helped lead Elvis to Christ tonight!"

"But Debbie, Elvis is dead."

I filled him in, and together we are still amazed at how God orchestrates things that we usually don't even give him the credit for. Oh yes . . . he not only made us, he loves us, and created us for a bigger story than just our own. We get to be part of his plan. And he values us enough to come after us with his love! Jesus esteemed Ernie the Elvis impersonator as a treasure and worth more than anyone could imagine.

As I pondered over the connecting of life dots, I was amazed that a car accident that was only a distant memory and a large scar on my leg were being used by God's hand twenty years later! Who would have ever thought? But God uses everything, and I was beginning to see this in true living color. I was also seeing how God loves and values people like Ernie. He values us so much that he goes to great lengths to bring us to himself and answer our prayers when we are searching. This one night in Las Vegas taught me more about this God we call "Father" than almost anything else in my memory. Why? Look at all the connecting dots declaring a sovereign, loving God! Yes, God values those he has made—he values us enough to come after us in his love.

God's Work Is Under Construction

Even though we are part of his glorious plan, we are still under construction. Once we recognize that this doesn't change our value or usefulness we can rest there. This year my husband and I went on a trip to Maui. We were so excited, and when we got to our room we were happy with everything. I quickly went to the lanai to see what kind of view we had and was awed by the beauty as I looked straight ahead. But when I turned my head to the right I realized there was something very different in my viewfinder. It was a construction site! And it was a mess!

All week I saw not only the beauty of Hawaii but also the disorder of a construction site. It was a wonderful reminder that God is working on me day and night, restoring me, rebuilding me, and creating beauty in me. All of this because he values that which he has made.

While we were there I also had many mornings of life lessons with the birds. The passages of Matthew and Luke became my marinade for the week.

> I tell you, do not worry about your life, what you will eat or drink; or about your body, what you will wear. Is not life more important

than food, and the body more important than clothes? Look at the birds of the air; they do not sow or reap or store away in barns, and yet your heavenly Father feeds them. Are you not much more valuable than they?

Matthew 6:25–26

Are not five sparrows sold for two pennies? Yet not one of them is forgotten by God. Indeed, the very hairs of your head are all numbered. Don't be afraid; you are worth more than many sparrows.

Luke 12:6

I kept seeing how God provided for the sparrows. Then one day as we came up from the beach we saw a little sparrow by our room. He was trying to fly out through the glass and beating his little head on the glass, trying to break through. Just behind him there was the open air and a whole sky to fly away in, but he was lost and just banging his head against the glass.

I thought of how many years I spent banging my head on the glass. I had tried to do it my way. I thought I could see where I was going, but there was a very real barrier in my way. Freedom was very close to me, just over my shoulder, but I just kept banging my silly head against the glass.

We named this little lost sparrow Sammy. Later, as we went out for dinner, Sammy Sparrow was still there. He wasn't beating against the glass anymore, because he was too tired. Instead he was curled up in the corner, having resigned himself to being lost. He could have flown away. Freedom was within reach. He just didn't realize it.

Is that how it is with you sometimes? Freedom is within your reach, but you are so exhausted that you just curl up in your corner and wait for a better day. Life has beaten you down and your thoughts about life, God, and yourself are not precious—they are painful. Well, the new day has come. It's time to cast down all thoughts that do not line up with truth and begin to breathe in the new fresh air of who you are in Christ.

Here is some truth to take in:

All things were created by him and for him.

Colossians 1:16

You are worthy, our Lord and God, to receive glory and honor and power, for you created all things, and by your will they were created and have their being.

Revelation 4:11

Listen to me . . . you whom I have upheld since you were conceived, and have carried since your birth. Even to your old age and gray hairs I am he, I am he who will sustain you. I have made you and I will carry you.

Isaiah 46:3–4

Know that the Lord is God. It is he who made us, and we are his.

Psalm 100:3

You and I are his very own. It is this truth alone that can change our lives forever, a system of belief that can cause faith to ignite within us. When faith comes alive within us, we begin to live differently. "Being his" is more than a phrase, it's a belief.

Telling Ourselves the Truth

"Our lives hold meaning because God loves us and because we are his. Our lives do not depend upon someone else loving us, staying with us, respecting us, noticing us, or pledging their eternal devotion to us."[6] We must recognize the truth, reconciling it for ourselves, and then find ways to remember it daily. Reconciling the truth is making friendship with it and accepting that it applies to us personally. When we recognize, reconcile, and remember, our lives change.

Believing we have value is a faith choice. It is saying that I am going to believe that what I read in Scripture is true. It is recognizing a value that is not based on conditions but on God and God alone. It is a sacrificial value that cost the blood of Christ. It is a new way to believe. Part of learning to believe is the exercise of speaking truth—telling ourselves the truth. When we are tempted to go to a negative place, it's important that we make a U-turn and tell ourselves the truth of God's love and care for us. Tell yourself the truth that you are valuable to God; you have worth to your creator. Tell yourself the truth that you do not have to worry but that you can give your cares, feelings, and concerns to him—and that he cares enough to listen and respond!

Remember you have a very real enemy who desires to rip you apart with lies. Don't forget that he is the father of lies, so lying is what he is expert at. If he can get you to buy into the non-truth about you, he can enslave you to yourself and your self-rejection and doubts. If he can convince you to define yourself by a faulty definition he will succeed in spoiling your life with flesh-induced choices, actions, and reactions. This is his plan. That is why we see in Scripture the need to cast down every thought that is not in line with truth.

> For though we live in the world, we do not wage war as the world does. The weapons we fight with are not the weapons of the world. On the contrary, they have divine power to demolish strongholds. We demolish arguments and every pretension that sets itself up

against the knowledge of God, and we take captive every thought to make it obedient to Christ.

2 Corinthians 10:3–5

Our weapons are the truth of God's Word. It isn't how the world views things, and if we are ever going to be transformed, we will have to make a choice to wrap our mind around the truth and ask God to make it alive to us. The peace we have in Christ refers to something happening inside of us; it's a peace of an internal order, not based on circumstances or the external order of the world. We must stand up to the lies.

Turning Trash to Treasure

As a young pastor's wife I led a weekly study called Design for Living, with a theme verse of John 10:10. I used to envision having days where women could come to "spiritual school" to learn spiritual disciplines and grow in Christ. But that dream dried up along with the ink on the divorce papers.

Before I moved away, my friends at the church gave me a manila envelope with the Design for Living logo and all info pertaining to our study. I refused to take it, saying, "This is the church's women's ministry." But they told me, "Debbie, this is your vision, and someday the Lord will use it again." I politely took it but thought to myself, *No way—God will never use me again!* I went home and threw the envelope in the trash, just knowing that God was through with me.

But sixteen years later God took Design for Living out of that trash can and rebirthed the vision. On a beautiful August weekend in 2005 the first Design4Living Spiritual Growth Conference was held in Livermore, California. Cornerstone Fellowship was filled with women and with some of my favorite speakers from all over the country. To top it all off—the Friday night kickoff concert featured Amy Grant. I was near tears the whole weekend. The tears were tears of joy as I was so tenderly reminded of a God who takes our trash and turns it, redeems it, makes it something for his purpose. Yes, he takes trash and transforms it into treasure!

This past summer at the second Design4Living Conference, our theme was "Living Intentionally—Choose Truth. Experience Change." We had conference shirts and hats that said "Choose Truth" on them. Shortly after the conference I went over to my neighbor's house for a brief visit. She greeted me at the front door, wearing her choose truth hat and shirt. Her husband got a kick out of all this and asked me, "What is all this 'choose truth' stuff about? Did you put on a liar's convention?" We all got a good laugh. Imagine putting on a liar's convention for women to learn how not to lie! But actually, teaching women to not listen to lies is a pretty good idea. In fact—it's key.

We are lied to by the father of lies on a regular basis. If he can keep us stuck in lies and painful unscriptural beliefs about ourselves, then he has successfully managed to steal from us the good that God came to give us. Remember, when we are stuck in ourselves, we are not in tune to God's voice in our lives.

The Lies:

My value depends on: beauty; success; talent; being pretty, perfect, and polished; what I have; what I do; if I am liked by people; having a good life.

I must constantly work at bettering "me": measuring up; being perfect because God only blesses and loves the good.

Everyone else: is happy; has a great life, marriage, kids, etc.; is loveable, desired, and wanted.

Nobody else: struggles the way I do.

What are your lies? What do you tell yourself? In *Telling Yourself the Truth*, the authors give the following exercise:

> Write in your notebook the things you tell yourself about yourself every day. Listen to your thoughts and your words. Remember, any thoughts that reflect hopelessness, desperation, hate, fear, bitterness, jealousy, or envy are the words and thoughts generated by demonic falsehood. These are words and thoughts that you will be changing and eliminating from your life.[7]

There is a very real battle, and God intends to give us victory and abundance by flooding us with truth. Truth frees our minds from the way of the world that we have become so accustomed to. Truth can give us a new definition, but first we must be aware that our old definitions may be big fat lies meant to keep us from accepting ourselves as God's beloved. The name "beloved" signifies tenderness, worth, and value. Believe this truth:

He is still saying, "Come . . ."

Come away with me.

Come to a place of freedom.

Come learn to trust that I hold the pieces of your life.

Come learn to trust that I value you, cherish you, and call you my own.

Come to me and learn how to live and walk in the truth.

Come and believe your new position in me.

For Further Reflection

1. Read Psalm 139:17–18. Have you ever counted sand? Imagine holding a handful of sand. Feel the grains across your

palm. Do you think you could pick the grains apart piece by piece and count them? What message does this give you about your value to God?

2. First Peter 2:9–10 states some important things about our value. Your title is "royalty." How can that change your view of yourself? Your positioning is "a people belonging to God." How can that give you a sense of belonging and value?

3. According to 1 Peter, you and I are called to declare God's praises. How can this be translated into a new purpose?

4. We also see in 1 Peter that . . . you once were . . . and you now are . . . Do you realize that you once were something different than you are now that you are in Christ?

5. What does a biblical concept of self-worth look like? Is it more about us or about God? What old beliefs or lies need to be removed in order to live in a biblical view of ourselves and our lives?

Step 3

Getting Reset for Living Differently

Moving to the Heartbeat of God in the Rhythm of Ordinary Life

Those who live should no longer live for themselves but for him who died for them.

2 Corinthians 5:15

To reorder one's own world, the need to simplify is imperative. Otherwise, we will find ourselves unable to be at rest within, unable to enter the deep, silent recesses of our hearts, where God's best messages are communicated. And if we live very long in that condition, our hearts grow cold toward Christ and we become objects of seduction in a wayward world.

Chuck Swindoll

Set

to put in a particular position. To become firm, secure, or fixed. To establish and settle. To cause to begin.

Many of us need an adjustment. If we are to line up to healthy belief and life-transforming truth, we must be reset. How do we get reset? By first getting real—because we cannot change anything that we haven't first acknowledged. Then by getting back to the essentials of faith. Truth sets us free, and going back to truth and exposing the lies of our past, our flesh, and our culture is a starting point.

From those starting points we begin to become firm, secure, and fixed as we learn how to manage our lives by faith and carry an attitude of praise into our daily circumstances. The core truths we have been soaking in are valuable, but responding to them is just as valuable. As we learn to respond to God's love and truth we will begin to be reset in a life of surrender and sacrifice. In this place God can do anything and everything through us as his cleansed vessel. It's a daily surrender, a moment by moment sacrifice, and a new way to live.

10

Choosing a New Direction

*Attitude Determines
the Music of the Heart*

A state of mind that sees God in everything is evidence of growth
in grace and a thankful heart.

Charles Finney

Does your life ever seem out of control? Mine too. There are many
things in life we can't control. Try as we may, some things are just
clearly out of our ability to change.

We don't get to know the answer to every "why?" and we can't
control other people or things that are out of our reach. But there
are two things we can do—each and every day. Each day we do
have control over:

163

1. The direction we will take.
2. The attitude we will have.

The children of Israel were given a charge to make a choice, and this charge is applicable to our lives today:

Choose for yourselves this day whom you will serve.

Joshua 24:15

I have set before you life and death, blessings and curses. Now choose life, so that you and your children may live and that you may love the LORD your God, listen to his voice, and hold fast to him. For the LORD is your life.

Deuteronomy 30:19–20

If I have learned anything over the past several years, it is how out of control life can be. I have been disappointed more times than I can count and have faced health issues, personal rejection, financial woes, worry over my children's futures, and many more things—too many to count.

I have also become convinced that making a daily choice regarding direction and attitude is *huge* in learning to walk in the Spirit. Unfortunately, I had to learn this the hard way!

A Lesson in Trusting God's Control

The months leading up to finalizing our divorce were long and lonely. Everything in my personal life went from bad to worse. My widowed mother, who worked at our church, had a stroke. I found myself nursing my wounded heart and my mother's ailing body.

To get away, I often made the long drive to my sister's house, five hours north of me. Her home became an oasis. As I was getting ready to leave after one visit, I took a quick spin to a local drugstore for some snacks for the ride home. I took my little four-year-old with me, and as we entered the store I picked him up to place him in the seat of the shopping cart.

As I lifted Cameron, I began to experience the most intense back pain I had ever felt. Within a few moments I passed out. The next thing I remember was waking up to a crowd around me and my little four-year-old looking at me with his big brown eyes, saying, "Mommy, are you gonna die?"

I tried to move my body, but it wasn't cooperating. Tears began to run down my cheeks, and my thoughts went all over the place. *What happened? What's wrong with me?* When the paramedics arrived they had to begin cutting through my clothes to determine what was going on. Having my clothes cut off in public was not the worst thing—getting sick and passing out every time they tried to move me was. I was strapped in and transported to the local hospital. My body was motionless, but my mind was going a mile a minute with thoughts like, *Am I going to be an invalid? What will happen to my little boys? How could so much happen to one person in such a short time? Oh no, this really can't be happening!*

Eventually I was released from the Northern California hospital and returned home. I was instructed to "rest" and allow the back injury some time to settle down before more testing to determine a course of treatment. There was a possibility that I had severely ruptured something and some talk of permanent nerve damage. Talk about out of control!

The people in our church took good care of me. They brought meals, took the boys for outings, and prayed for us. One particular afternoon I was so angry that I thought I would burst, and as soon as everyone left to take the kids to the neighborhood park, I did burst. I began to pray out loud, "Okay, Lord, what could you be thinking? Going through life with a severe injury that could possibly cost me my ability to raise my little boys . . . well, this is over the top and so unfair! I am so upset. I'm not sure that I believe anything anymore. Where is your love? What about your protection? Where in the world are you now? Is this what I get for spending over ten years serving you in the ministry? I was trying to do the right thing! Trying to be good! I tried to be a good wife and look at what I got. Now I just want to raise my boys and be a good mother, and I can't even move. I don't understand, Lord, I just don't understand."

Suddenly three numbers flashed across the screen of my mind: 8-2-8. Those three numbers were like a neon light in my thoughts, and I knew what they meant but wasn't willing to believe it.

As a young pastor's wife I had the privilege of knowing three older women who were mentors to me. Of course, back then we didn't call it mentoring, it was just friendship—the older walking alongside the younger. For many years, Becky, Jinny, and Mary Lou walked alongside me and poured spiritual lessons into my life in too many ways to count. But it was Jinny's insistence on the truth of Romans 8:28 that came back to me now in my time of crisis and confusion.

A few years before my divorce, Jinny was going through a very hard time, and she held on to the promise represented in those three numbers like they were life itself. I remember once when we were in her minivan and the digital clock read 8:28. "Debbie, look at that, 8-2-8, you know what that means, don't you?" Well, I was just thinking, *Yeah, 8:28 in the morning,* but Jinny had another version of the significance of the clock's numbers. She quickly said, "Romans 8:28 tells us that all things work together for those who love God and are called for his purpose."

I thought, *How nice, Jinny is trying to cheer herself up.*

On one occasion we were at the grocery store when the clerk rang up $8.28. Jinny exclaimed with glee, "8-2-8!" The clerk looked at us and asked, "Is something wrong with the price?" Jinny chimed in with a smile, "Oh no, 8-2-8 is a promise in God's Word that says all things work together for good." And even I, the spiritual little pastor's wife, thought Jinny was clearly over the top.

But the real clincher was one hot August morning when Jinny called my house and asked, "Do you know what today is?"

"Um . . . Thursday?"

"Yes, it's Thursday, and it's 8-28. All things work together for good because we are called by God and he is sovereign over our lives."

I must admit I wanted to scream. But I loved Jinny so very much and I was politely glad that the verse was helping her through a very hard time. Believe me when I say that I just didn't "get it" back then.

So there I was a few years later going through the breakup of my marriage and lying in my bed, unable to walk without assistance. I was crying out to God, and those numbers kept blinking in my mind. Ugh!

"Lord, you can't really expect me to believe this *now*, can you?" And all I got were those three numbers again. Like Chinese water torture, those three numbers kept tapping against my mind—*8-2-8 . . . 8-2-8 . . . 8-2-8 . . . 8-2-8 . . .*

"Okay, Lord!" I cried out. Now reduced to tears, I prayed between sobs. "How can I possibly believe this? The marriage is bad enough, but what about my back? I thought you would help me provide for me and my kids, but now it looks like I won't be able to take care of us. How do you expect me to handle this?"

And I will never forget what happened next as long as I live. It wasn't an audible voice, but it was a message from deep within me, a sure thought penetrating me from the core. I believed it was a clear message to me from God: *Especially your back—trust me.*

I cried myself to sleep that afternoon, and when I woke up I had an incredible peace. I suddenly realized it was that peace that passes understanding that I used to sing about in church. I had no idea what the Lord meant by "*Especially your back—trust me,*" but I knew that God had touched me that afternoon.

Within a few weeks I was walking again and never needed surgery. It was later confirmed through MRI testing that I had indeed ruptured two discs in my back and was very fortunate that they healed without surgical intervention. Things weren't perfect, but I kept holding on to those three numbers that I had previously secretly mocked. My motto became "8-2-8."

That promise reads,

And we know that in all things God works for the good of those who love him, who have been called according to his purpose.

But look at the next verse,

For those God foreknew he also predestined to be conformed to the likeness of his Son.

Romans 8:29

I was clearly getting the picture. God takes all things and works good out of them, and the good that comes out of them is the purifying of our lives that we might become more like Jesus.

I like this story told by Max Lucado.

God loves you just the way you are, but he refuses to leave you that way. He wants you to be just like Jesus. When my daughter Jenna was a toddler, I used to take her to a park not far from our apartment. One day as she was playing in a sandbox, an ice-cream salesman approached us. I purchased her a treat, and when I turned to give it to her, I saw her mouth was full of sand. Where I intended to put a delicacy, she had put dirt.

Did I love her with dirt in her mouth? Absolutely. Was she any less my daughter with dirt in her mouth? Of course not. Was I going to allow her to keep the dirt in her mouth? No way. I loved her right where she was, but I refused to leave her there. I carried her over to the water fountain and washed out her mouth. Why? Because I love her.

God does the same for us. He holds us over the fountain. "Spit out the dirt, honey," the Father urges. "I've got something better for you." And so he cleanses us of filth: immorality, dishonesty, prejudice, bitterness, greed. We don't enjoy the cleansing; sometimes we even opt for the dirt over the ice cream. "I can eat dirt if I want to!" we pout and proclaim. Which is true—we can. But if we do, the loss is ours. God has a better offer. He wants us to be just like Jesus.[1]

God loved me too much to leave me the way I was. I was fake and never realized it until my life fell apart. In that broken place, with all the props and securities pulled, I had to find out firsthand what was real. God in his goodness allowed me not just one strike but three—and like they say at the ballpark, I was out. Little did I know that the back incident was the very circumstance that God allowed that would later lead me to my future husband.

The Pieces of Our Lives

Over the years I have learned to look at life in a new way. When you purchase a jigsaw puzzle, the box has a wonderful picture on the top. But when you open the box there are hundreds and sometimes thousands of pieces that look nothing like the picture.

They look like a heap of odd-shaped pieces that could never fit together. But every little piece in that box counts. Each piece, no matter how irregular, has its purpose and place as part of the overall picture.

So it is with us. Our lives are like one big puzzle that at times seems impossible to make sense of. But unlike with the jigsaw puzzle, we have no idea what the finished picture is. The good news is that God does. Our Creator, who formed us in our mother's womb, who wrote our days in his book before one of them came to be, knows the planned picture of our lives. He also knows that some of the misshapen pieces are necessary parts of the puzzle. And so it was with the black piece of my back incident.

After I started recovering and gaining strength, I began visiting my sister in Northern California again. This one particular week I traveled with some friends to a Christian seminar at the Oakland Coliseum. I stayed at my sister's house so she could take care of the boys, while my friends stayed at their relatives' house across town. Each morning we met for coffee and pastries and made the thirty-minute drive to Oakland. I must admit that I felt a bit like a zombie at each session, but it felt good to at least be trying to connect to life again.

The morning of the last session my friend Mary called me and told me not to go with them on that Saturday morning. She was concerned that the day's topic—marriage—might be uncomfortable for me. I agreed.

Now I had a problem. What was I going to do all day with the boys? My sister got called into work, so I began to feel a bit panicked because I still needed help just to manage through a day.

My sister once again saved the day with a plan. "There's a parade downtown. Why don't you take the boys? All kids love parades. But you better hurry; it starts in about an hour."

I quickly woke up the boys and packed the car to go to the parade. We were pretty wrinkled, very tired, and definitely disoriented. We arrived early, but I was glad because we had our pick of the street spots. I settled in with the boys on the corner of St. Mary's Street and Main Street, right in front of an old-fashioned and charming-looking gas station. Before long a man and two little girls came and put their things next to ours.

The little girls immediately began conversing with the boys, and the four hit it off in seconds. It seemed like they were all friends. Realizing that they too were early, their father went into Mr. Dad mode and began playing with all four kids. A bubble gum contest broke out, followed by snacks and drinks. I was happy that someone was entertaining my kids. God had provided. I didn't say a word to any of them but instead just slumped down in my little folding chair, with my big sunglasses hiding my pain. I was content in the moment because my boys were safe and having fun.

The parade itself was a blur, and I don't remember it starting or ending. But before I knew it everyone was packing up. I had enough sense to tell my children to thank the nice man for the gum and drinks. I took their hands and walked them up to Mr. Dad, and they did just that. Justin and Cameron both politely thanked him for the gum, treats, and drinks, and Mr. Dad smiled and looked right into my sunglass-covered eyes and said, "I know this is Justin, and this is Cameron, and you are?"

"Oh, I'm Debbie. Thank you so much for entertaining the kids."

"Are you just Debbie, or do you have a last name?"

Startled by that question, I popped off, "I'm just Debbie, I don't have a last name!" Then I did the funniest thing—I turned and ran away as fast as my legs would take me while holding onto two little boys and a beach chair. It must have been quite a sight to see a crazed-looking mom darting in and out of the crowds on Main Street.

The boys were over the top about their morning and began telling my sister as soon as they saw her. "Auntie Sharon, we met Magnum P.I. and his girls!" My sister smiled and with raised eyebrows asked, "Magnum P.I.?"

Flustered I quickly responded, "No, of course not Magnum P.I.! We just met some guy at the parade, and he had two little girls that were the same ages as the boys."

Smiling again she said, "Well, maybe he'll look you up."

"No, don't worry. He asked if I had a last name, and I said no and ran down the street like I had seen a ghost."

We got a good laugh.

But the boys would not quit talking about them. Once we got home they were telling people that they'd met Magnum P.I. and his girls. Friend after friend smiled and said, "Maybe he'll look you up."

Finally fed up, I blew up one day. "What does everyone not get about this? I didn't actually meet a man, my kids did. I didn't have any real contact with him. I ran when he asked me my name. And besides, I don't want anyone to look me up. I already told the Lord that I'll be alone forever unless he clearly plops someone into my life. The end!"

Weeks went by, and the boys asked things like, "When we go to see Auntie Sharon, are we going to see the girls?"

"No, we are not going to see the girls."

"Why not, Mommy?"

"We don't know the girls. We don't know those people. We are never seeing them again!"

So you can bet I was shocked when five weeks after the parade I got a phone call. "I don't know if you'll remember me, but my daughters and I met you and your sons at the Alameda County Fair Parade." I'm surprised I didn't faint.

There was an awkward silence on my end, so he quickly began apologizing. "I'm sorry if this call is inappropriate. I don't even know if you're single. I just thought . . ."

"Well," I began, "I'm a Christian. And I'm going through a horrible time. I don't believe in divorce. I'm not happy about it, and I have no interest in meeting anyone else ever!"

Quick to apologize he continued, "I'm a Christian too. And a few years ago I went through a very painful divorce. I didn't think I would make it through, so I understand. Let me give you my number. If you're ever in the area again and just need to talk to someone who has been through it, you can give me a call."

I scribbled the number on a scratch pad, politely said good-bye, and hung up the phone. I was stunned the rest of the day. Then it hit me . . . how did he get my number? I had said I had no last name!

I called the number back and got a recording machine. "Hi, this is Debbie. I need to know how you got my number."

The Other Side of the Story

The man my kids were calling Magnum P.I. had a real name—Ray. His wife left him a few years earlier, and the divorce eventually drove him to his knees, and he accepted Christ at Hume Lake Christian Camp. He had done the dating scene, and it had left him empty. So he began to pray that God would bring a strong Christian woman into his life, for him and his daughters. That seems hilarious to me now, because I certainly was not the picture of a strong Christian woman in those days.

The second part of his prayer was, "Lord, when I meet her, I pray that I will know it's her."

That day at the parade while I was oblivious to his presence, he felt I was the one he had been praying for. But when I said I didn't have a last name and ran down the street, he had a problem. "Lord, if it's her, how do I find her?"

Well, he wasn't Magnum P.I., but he was a real detective. But even good detectives can't find someone without a trail or some clues, and I left him neither.

He talked to his police buddies and told them he had to find me. He suspected I lived out of the area and thought of putting a billboard up on Hwy. 5 that said "Met you and your boys at the Alameda County Fair Parade . . . Call Ray."

"Ray, do you know how many crazy girls will call you? Besides, you have no problem getting a date. What's up? Was she just really gorgeous?"

To which he replied, "I have no idea what she looks like. She had these huge sunglasses on and never really interacted with me." His friends were clearly confused. He knew they wouldn't understand even if he tried explaining.

After weeks of being convinced that he had to find me and weeks of no clue how, he was just about ready to give up. Then one final prayer: "Lord, if I am supposed to find this woman and if it is you that is putting this on my heart, you are going to have to show me how."

After that prayer, as he was drifting off to sleep, he flashed on something my little Cameron had said during the parade that was clearly a clue. At small-town parades, an ambulance is often included as a sort of float, and Cameron was very excited to see an ambulance again. So excited that when he saw it he exclaimed, "The last time we were here my mommy broke her back and got to ride in an ambulance." There it was! A clue! She had been in a local accident . . . Ray went to sleep that night knowing that he was going to find me.

He was able to find out that there was a Debbie who had been taken by ambulance from Pleasanton months earlier, but there was no phone number, just a street address. Calling directory assistance proved to be a dead end as the number was not listed. As a last-ditch resort he decided to call the police department in the city I lived in, not as a business call but as a personal one, to see if he could get any cross-reference help. He felt a little embarrassed about doing this, so it took a few days to gather enough courage.

The day came. He made the call, and before he could even go into his planned speech, a voice on the other end began to get excited.

"Ray, Ray, this is Brenda!" Brenda was his cousin. He had no idea that she worked there, and no idea she lived in that city.

"What are you doing there?"

"I work here."

She listened to his story, as confused as everyone else who'd heard it before her, and looked up the number.

So that's how Ray got my number. And he called me back the same night I left the message on his answering machine. He was polite, sweet, and gentle. He was also scared that I would think he was a lunatic for tracking me down. Funny thing is, once he called we began talking about something else, and I completely forgot to ask him how he found me. In fact, I didn't ask for quite awhile. Believe it or not, I forgot about it. The friendship with Ray was just a nonthreatening phone friendship. It seemed natural, and in no time at all he became someone I could connect with about my personal pain. I began to see this new long-distance friend as someone who had been through what I was going through. Neither of us believed in divorce. We both loved our kids with everything in us. I'm glad that Ray didn't initially tell me about his prayer or how he felt when he met me, because I was only drawn to him in friendship at first. But a little over a year later, we were married with our children as our attendants. That was eighteen years ago.

Remember when God spoke to me and said, "*Especially your back—trust me*"?

At the time, the back incident was a very black piece of the puzzle of my life's picture. At the time it happened, it seemed to be the worst possible thing that could have taken place in my life. I didn't understand it. I was mad about it, and to me it was the last straw. But without it, everything would have been different. It was the very piece of information that Ray needed to find me many months later. And had God not literally plopped Ray into my life, I never would have made it in a second marriage.

Blending our families was very hard at first, but time and time again, we remembered how God had brought us together, and we just hung in there, knowing that even this tough blended family life was going to turn out to be one of those "all things work together for good." And it has. I still am in awe of God's hand in the pieces of life—yes, even the dark ones.

I am convinced that we are all part of a greater story and that life is a much bigger picture than we realize. When we learn to live according to the bigger picture, life is different. Our circumstances may not change, but we change. When our focus is on the end result that God knows, we begin to live by faith and not by what we can see. In this place it begins to make sense to praise God in every situation we find ourselves in.

> Be joyful always; pray continually; give thanks in all circumstances, for this is God's will for you in Christ Jesus.
>
> 1 Thessalonians 5:16–18

Why are we told to give thanks in all circumstances? Notice it doesn't say "for" but "in." We can give thanks because God is good, and he is working out all things for our good and his glory. So in everything we can give thanks. The key word is *in*. We are "in" Christ, so "in" every circumstance we can learn to live life ruled by a bigger picture.

The illustration of the puzzle can teach us a lot about where our focus is. And our focus determines the attitude and direction we will take each day.

In the Box Living—Self Focus

Believing that the pieces of the puzzle don't make sense.

Viewing hardships in a merely negative light.

Being defeated by failure/weakness.

Letting circumstances become your thermometer.

Waiting for the "perfect" situation in order to submit to God.

Out of the Box Living—Faith Focus

Understanding that God sees the finished product, and that every piece of the puzzle is designed to fit (8-2-8).

Learning that hardships produce growth and eventual good.

Letting your failure/weakness cause dependence on God.

Not letting your circumstances become an emotional trigger.

Taking daily steps despite my "not so perfect" situation.

Trusting that things happen to you so that something can happen in you.

Big Picture Living—Eternal Focus

Recognizing that God knows the plan.

Realizing that he guides the path.

Relying on his greater good and purpose.

Keeping your focus fixed on the truth that everything is about a bigger picture, and God knows that picture.

Choosing a new direction is an important step. For me, praising God in all things was certainly new. It felt foreign and uncomfortable, but true to God's Word it gave me peace. I began the journey of being thankful in all things. Even now, I forget many times and have to remind myself after my attitude starts spinning out of control. But when I come back to the attitude of praise, my perspective reverts to the bigger picture. Ahh . . . yes, God is indeed in control—he knows me, he protects me, he made me, and he values me. I can take a stand to be on his side, and I can surrender all! Praise God for his faithfulness in our lives. We really *can* learn to get over ourselves—and the attitude of praise is part of the process.

Again the Lord is bidding us, "Come close . . ."

Come to me with all your pieces—big pieces, small pieces, it doesn't matter the size or shape. I am in them all.

Come to me for faith.

Come to me with a thankful heart.

Come to me in praise, even when you don't understand, knowing that I do.

Come believe that I exist and I reward those who seek me.

Come to me and let me be your living reality.

178

For Further Reflection

1. What seems out of control about life? What, if anything, can you control?
2. Joshua 24:15 encourages choice. What can you choose each day?
3. What does 8-2-8 mean to you? Have you ever considered it in context with 8-2-9? In context, what does it say to you about your life, your problems, and your pain?
4. Can you praise God about all the pieces of your life? How would remembering that God knows the bigger picture help you in making it through the hard times?

11

Choosing a Life of Dependence

We Can't Control the Length, Only the Depth

Man's days are determined; you have decreed the number of his months and have set limits he cannot exceed.

Job 14:5

We have looked at the four core truths of Psalm 139:

He knows me.

He protects me.

He made me.

He values me.

But Psalm 139 doesn't end with those four core truths. The rest of Psalm 139 is just as meaningful, as it holds the key to unlock how we will live out our lives as God's children. The next few verses can appear to be random and out of order, but as we take a closer look, it's clear to see that it is David's response to the truth of God's love for him. I call this "Love's Response" because it is a response to the truth. It is not enough to hear and know the truth—we must respond to the truth.

Take a look with me:

> If only you would slay the wicked, O God!
> Away from me, you bloodthirsty men!
> They speak of you with evil intent;
> your adversaries misuse your name.
> Do I not hate those who hate you, O LORD,
> and abhor those who rise up against you?
> I have nothing but hatred for them;
> I count them my enemies.
>
> Psalm 139:19–22

Whoa! Where did all that come from? After proclaiming God's unending involvement in his life and God's love and protection, David launches into a different direction—or does he?

Let me ask you a question. When you know somebody loves you, really loves you, and is totally devoted to you—what is your response to that kind of love? For me, my response is to reciprocate that love; simply put, to love them back. And when I really love somebody I want to stand on their side, defend them, hold them up, and protect them. In other words, I want to love what they love and hate what they hate—becoming part of them. Now apply that kind of response to the marvelous love God has for us, and it's easy to see that David was responding to God's love by making a firm stand. I want to hate those who hate you, Lord, for I am now on your side—in the camp of the Lord God!

This is a key to how the core truths can change our lives as they become our belief system. As our thoughts line up with God's Word and our hearts are more secure in the truth of his love, our relationship with him takes on a whole new dimension. We are not just "believers." We become lovers of Jesus, people who are on his side of the fence. No more straddling the line, no more mediocrity—we want everything he has for us, and we will change directions to get that, if changing directions is what's necessary.

Psalm 139:19–22 is Love's Response—which is our surrender to all God has for us.

> **Surrender**: to give up control or possession of to another. To give oneself over; to yield.

In order to surrender I had to radically change directions. My attitude about life had gotten so out of control that every part of me was dying a slow death. I hated my attitude but felt a victim to it. The entrance of these core truths of God's love for me into my belief system began to rearrange how I thought about everything. It caused me to take a new path. I was discovering that I was indeed someone different. I was reveling in the truth that I was filled with the power and presence of God's Holy Spirit. I was new! I was his creation! This positioning gave me purpose. And having purpose was igniting a passion in me like none that I had ever experienced. And this passion was giving me the desire to stand on his side—whatever the cost.

I was being called out by God to live differently, not because it would earn me spiritual brownie points but because I was different and it was time for my identity in Christ to line up with my reality on earth.

In the book of Romans the apostle Paul tells us about surrender too. He calls it being a living sacrifice.

For from him and through him and to him are all things. To him be the glory forever! Amen. Therefore, I urge you, brothers, in view of God's mercy, to offer your bodies as living sacrifices, holy and pleasing to God—this is your spiritual act of worship. Do not conform any longer to the pattern of this world, but be transformed by the renewing of your mind. Then you will be able to test and approve what God's will is—his good, pleasing and perfect will.

Romans 11:36–12:2

Eugene Peterson calls it giving your life as an offering:

Everything comes from him; Everything happens through him; Everything ends up in him. Always glory! Always praise! Yes. Yes. Yes. So, here's what I want you to do, God helping you: Take your everyday, ordinary life—your sleeping, eating, going-to-work, and walking-around life—and place it before God as an offering. Embracing what God does for you is the best thing you can do for him. Don't become so well-adjusted to your culture that you fit into it without even thinking. Instead, fix your attention on God. You'll be changed from the inside out.

Romans 11:36–12:2 Message

Each of us gets to choose how much of us we will open up to God. He is there, but he is always saying "Come to me." And each day we get to choose if we will or we won't. Do you want to go deeper? Well, you can. It's really up to you.

A true turning point for me came when I made a decision to forgive. I can remember telling my counselor that I was so afraid that my boys would never grow up to know Jesus.

184

"After all," I reasoned, "their father was a pastor."

"Well, then, Debbie, it's now up to you."

"Up to me? I didn't want to be divorced. I didn't want the kids to hurt like this!"

"Maybe not. But you will hurt them now if you allow the bitterness, hatred, and unforgiveness you are carrying to live in you much longer."

I was angry. But I wanted so desperately for my children to grow up with faith in God. I realized that leaving them a legacy of faith, hope, and love would be a worthwhile goal. Teaching them about broken people needing a powerful God would serve them well in the real world. And then God spoke to me . . . *Debbie, pastors are people, and people need the Lord. Their father didn't want to hurt them either, but life happened and you were all hurt in the process.* Suddenly the power of God's agape love began to flood me. I had to forgive. I had to let go and release all of the hurt to God. It was part of the faith walk that I now was responsible to live in. Just as God had made his love for me a new living reality, he made me realize that his love for my ex-husband was just as real. This man, the father of my children, was God's beloved. And, as God's own, he was in need of the grace of God just as much as I was.

If God knew me, protected me, made me, and valued me, then I had a responsibility to respond to that magnificent love. The choice to forgive was mine; the power that enabled the forgiveness to be real was God's. Jesus met me at the crossroads of love and hate and did a miracle in my heart. Now I am certain that my children will be left with the legacy of love, grace, and forgiveness.

And as the years have gone by, this legacy is also part of my stepdaughters' heritage too. If they were ever going to grow up knowing the love of Jesus, somewhere along the way a choice had to be made.

If it is possible, as far as it depends on you, live at peace with everyone.

Romans 12:18

Forgive, and you will be forgiven. Give, and it will be given to you. . . . For with the measure you use, it will be measured to you.

Luke 6:37–38

We all need to make the choice to simplify our lives. In the midst of the drama of daily living and the confusion of real-life relationships, it will serve us well to be reset for living with a simplified plan.

Look at these two passages:

"Love the Lord your God with all your heart and with all your soul and with all your mind." This is the first and greatest commandment. And the second is like it: "Love your neighbor as yourself."

Matthew 22:37–39

All things were created by him and for him.

Colossians 1:16

Here we go, girls—a new mission for life: I was created by God and for God's purposes, to love God and to love others. If I were to make a bumper sticker it would simply be: By God—For God . . . Love God—Love Others.

This is a new attitude, a new direction, and a new way to live. It's not about us. It's about the bigger picture. As I grew in faith and as my new journey continued, I realized that my relationship with God was taking on a new depth. It really wasn't about me as much anymore.

My story continues, and so does yours. We will be living out our stories until the day we take our last breath here on earth. God even knows the expiration date. My friend, when she found out she was dying, would tease about her expiration date and shelf life. Instead of feeling robbed of life, she knew her real life was the one to come. Truth is, though we can live healthier and happier, we can't live any longer than the day determined for us. This knowledge can bring tremendous peace, and it can also cause us to choose a different type of life—not wasting a moment. Can you see how learning to believe truth and trust God is a much better way to live?

It's exciting to know God and to learn to walk with him and trust him. I use the word *learn* because walking with him is not a given or an automatic. We must learn how to walk with him, and we must practice trusting him and embracing his Word.

Learning to manage our life by faith requires the foundation of understanding that we have worth because of God's signature on our lives and because of God's love for us. Once we recognize and take in the truth that he is involved with our entire life—past, present, and future—we begin to shift our thinking and learn to trust him with everything.

As time went on I had to learn a lot about trusting God for the bigger picture. Looking back, I can't believe how small my thinking used to be. I used to live as a victim and mull around in my little pieces of hurt, wanting to throw another dark jagged piece at someone else so they could hurt too. I didn't know how else to live. My life had always been based on what I felt, not what faith told me to do.

When I do a weekend retreat I usually close the session on faith by having the women come forward and take a puzzle piece from boxes that I put on the stage. Based on where they are in life, their piece will be significant for one of these reasons:

They need to surrender their lives to Christ for the very first time.

They need to let go of something like unforgiveness.

They need to release their frustration with the way life has turned out.

They need to learn to hope in the bigger picture.

They need to make a recommitment to living as his.

I watch as they go back to their seats, puzzle piece in hand. Some then kneel; others put their head in their hands; still others sing out songs of worship and freedom. All of them are different for having remembered the sovereignty of God, the plan of God, and the power of God to use all things to make us more like Jesus.

I close the session by telling them that the puzzle piece is to be a reminder. They are to put it somewhere that they will see it a lot over the next few weeks. Some put it on their computer monitors at home or work. Others put it on their bathroom mirror. Where it ends up doesn't matter. What does matter is that the puzzle piece serves as a reminder of Romans 8:28.

The other day I was in a local airport returning from an out-of-state speaking engagement. A woman ran toward me. I looked around to see if something was wrong but didn't see anything unusual. Then before I could turn around she was right in front of me.

Holding up a very worn little puzzle piece she said, "Remember this? I've carried it all year. It's reminded me to trust God with every piece of my life. And this year life has been hard. But you know what? I've learned that God really does use all things. Thank you for helping me see that life is like a bunch of pieces that God is using to form the bigger picture!" I hugged her because she was a sister of the heart. Both of us needed to learn that there are two things that we can control each day—and if we do, our life will begin to be managed by faith instead of fear or feelings.

Learning to Live Differently

Many times during the practice of our faith our steps feel clumsy. That's okay. For years we learned how to live by a different standard—the world's. Some of us took that same standard into our Christian life and continued having that as our belief system while filling our mind with spiritual information. It's kind of like knowing the calorie count of every food and knowing how to be your healthiest yet each day engaging in high-calorie living, which keeps you from experiencing the benefit of the information you know. So instead of fit—which you should be because you know how to be—you are fat, tired, and frustrated.

As Christians, we *know* what is required. We can even quote verses about what is required with confidence and ease. But do we learn to live and *do* what is required?

I remember one time when my counselor asked me a question after I had been talking about something that was frustrating to me.

"Debbie, do you think you could make it in this situation until 5:00 p.m.?"

Considering it was my lunch hour, I thought and said, "Yes, because I'm at work away from the chaos."

"Well, what about until 9:00 p.m.?"

I thought a little longer this time, scanning my brain for evening activities. "Yeah, because we'll be busy with schoolwork and getting everything done."

"What about until midnight?"

189

With this question I laughed out loud. "Of course, they'll all be in bed!"

Then he began to infuse me with some tools for reality living: "You know, Debbie, Jesus taught us that we are to live one day at a time."

"Oh yes," I interrupted, "I know, it's in Matthew chapter 6 . . ." And I rattled off the verse.

He patiently smiled. "Oh, I see . . . you know the verse and even where to find it, but have you ever tried living by those instructions from Christ himself?"

Oops! No, I hadn't ever tried that. How did I miss it? I knew the verse. I knew it was the words of Christ. I guess I just never took Scripture as seriously as I should have. How much else had I missed? I had been a Christian then for many years and realized that I had missed so much by taking Scripture for granted rather than digging into it as truth.

The deeper walk is about walking in who you are as a woman belonging to God. In this place your responsibility to truth is to learn to walk in the Spirit instead of the ways of the flesh.

With each event that takes place in our lives—from the smallest to the largest—we get to choose how to respond. Most of us haven't a conscious thought about our responses. But when we live as God's, we need to change this way of operating.

Our Response to Life

There is a process of dealing with circumstances that we have learned since we were young.

- Circumstance—something happens
- Perception of circumstance—how I view it

- Message about circumstance—what I tell myself about it
- Childish pattern as response to circumstance—how I handle it (pout, withdraw, manipulate, hide, lie, gossip, deflect, etc.)
- Comfort—what I use to fill myself or distract myself from the pain (people, food, alcohol, drugs, shopping, gossiping, etc.)

Living in the Flesh

- Life happens/circumstance
- I feel
- I act on my feelings in childish ways and choose flesh over the Spirit
- I am in bondage to the pattern of how I've always responded (for some this might be drowning in a pool of chocolate bars!)

We need to stop this pattern and instead live in the Spirit.

Living in the Spirit

- Life happens/circumstance
- I feel
- I pray and give any unpleasant anxiety or feelings to God
- I tell myself the truth (find verses to reinforce truth in every situation) and choose to believe the truth
- At first this is uncomfortable (it's easier to run to chocolate!)

Here are some things that can help us live in the Spirit.

- Find a verse that speaks to the situation
- Press into Jesus—pray the verse and claim the promise

- Praise God in the circumstance
- Go over the truth, repeat, remember, repeat
- Walk in the truth by faith—make new faith choices that are not based solely on emotion

It is uncomfortable to choose the Spirit because we are used to handling life by our own natural tendencies, habits, and patterns. I never realized how deeply ingrained habits could be until one weekend in a hotel in Southern California.

My friend and I had traveled to a speaking engagement. When we arrived we discovered that the hotel did not block out enough rooms for the retreat being held there. They sat me in the lobby and scrambled to figure out what to do. I was the guest speaker for the weekend, and they were more than embarrassed that they had no room at the inn!

It all worked out rather well because they put us in the penthouse on the top floor. Amazing. We danced around the giant floor plan like little girls, checking out the views and touching all the fancy furniture. But when I went to get a drink of cold water from the bathroom vanity, things went downhill.

"I can't believe that they don't have cold water in a fancy penthouse! Look, the faucet only delivers hot water," I said to my friend.

With a stunned look on her face, she said, "Debbie, you haven't even tried to use the right faucet on the sink. The right side has cold water." She pushed past me to prove her point, and the right faucet delivered.

I began to laugh out loud because I realized what had happened. Back home, the cold water spout on my bathroom sink had been broken for about eighteen months. When I first noticed the broken faucet, I told my husband, and he assured me he would get someone to fix it. I didn't want to be a nag, and certain it would get fixed, I devised my own way of handling the situation in the meantime.

Since it usually took a little while for the water to heat up, I would turn the faucet on, quickly clean my contacts, take my medication, and hurry and wash my face before the water was too hot to touch. At first I had to concentrate on what I was doing to get it all down. But after just a short time it became my new routine, or habit. Once the new pattern was ingrained, I didn't even think about it and forgot to nag my husband to get it fixed. That is until that night in the penthouse when I was standing in front of a fully functional sink and I was completely dysfunctional! It only takes twenty-one days to develop a habit. Most of us have habitual ways of living that reflect the flesh and not the Spirit life within us.

Things Happen to Us

None of us likes pain. Pain brings us to a place of dependence on God. It's not a fun place to be, but it is a necessary place if we are going to become all God has created us to be.

I have a saying that I use with each new test and trial: "Things happen to me so something can happen in me." And I believe this with all my heart.

> The testing of your faith develops perseverance. Perseverance must finish its work so that you may be mature and complete, not lacking anything.
>
> James 1:3–4

Things happen to us (tests, trials, hardships) so that something can happen in us (maturity, completeness).

C. S. Lewis said, "Pain is a megaphone." Those words couldn't be more descriptive or more accurate. Pain calls out to us, magnifying itself until it reaches us at the deepest level. We often don't want to go to this depth level, but we need to realize that the pain does have a purpose. And this purpose makes pain our friend—not usually an invited guest, but a friend nonetheless.

There are many types of pain—physical, emotional, and circumstantial. And when pain strikes up its band, my heart screams, "Hey, wait a minute, I want to be happy! I don't want to be in this place." Almost as quickly as I curse pain, I can hear an inner wisdom guiding my thoughts in another direction—to the purpose in the pain.

The apostle Paul gives us an example of one who experienced pain yet retrained his focus and dependence on God's love for him.

> We are hard pressed on every side, but not crushed; perplexed, but not in despair; persecuted, but not abandoned; struck down, but not destroyed. . . . We do not lose heart. Though outwardly we are wasting away, yet inwardly we are being renewed day by day. . . . So we fix our eyes not on what is seen, but on what is unseen. For what is seen is temporary, but what is unseen is eternal. . . . For Christ's love compels us . . . that those who live should no longer live for themselves but for him.
>
> 2 Corinthians 4:8–9, 16, 18; 5:14–15

Have you ever been pressed by pain?

I have, and at times it seems like only yesterday. I can remember the weather, the flowers that were blooming, and the deadness steadily taking over my heart. Life happened, turned my world upside down, and left me feeling suspended in midair. But in the story of my real life, the pain brought about something new and something real in my faith walk.

194

To my surprise my heart has grown stronger, warmer, and more pliable in the hands of God. I have confidence that this can happen for you too. If you are hurting and wondering what your pain is about—remember Jesus. He is working in you. I know it's hard, some days brutally hard, but something is happening in you. That is the promise of Romans 8:28–29.

Max Lucado simplifies it when he says, "He wants to make us just like Jesus."[1] That's it. The eternal crystallized. The pieces of the puzzle put together. The pain given purpose. We are being changed daily and being made into people we could never be without the brokenness of pain and disappointment. Oh yes, pain is a megaphone. Loud, harsh, calling us to listen, forcing us to attention, and in the end inspiring us to cheer.

The game is on. We are in the middle of the field, and we can't give up now. Let pain call you, draw you, inspire you to take heart and focus on the bigger picture . . . the unseen, eternal glory that far outweighs everything else.

Do you hear him calling you?

Come to me, and I will show you how to live.

Come to me, for I have the plan.

Come to me, for I know the purpose.

Come to me, for I am the one, the only one, who can turn dark into light again.

For Further Reflection

1. Read Psalm 139:19–22. This is Love's Response. How does this relate to you? What would it look like to take God's side, to stand in truth?

195

2. According to Luke 6:37–38, how would standing on his side, in truth, affect your relationships?

3. Does a simplified mission for life help you?

4. What is your current mission statement? How does it line up with "By God—For God . . . Love God—Love Others"?

5. What lifestyle habits are you stuck in that might prevent you from responding to God in lining up to truth?

12

Choosing to Make Each Day Count

Becoming the Everyday Vessel

> Yield yourself to His leading. We have seen that leading is not just in the mind or thoughts, but in the life and disposition. Yield yourself to God, to be guided by the Holy Spirit in all your conduct.
>
> Andrew Murray

Every day is a gift—to be opened, cherished, and lived fully. I haven't always realized the gift of each day. But over the years as new core truths have become more cemented into my reality, I see each day through a different lens. The beauty of living each day in God is that he does provide every resource that I need—if I stay connected to him as my source.

So far today, God,
I've done all right . . .
I haven't gossiped.
I haven't been grumpy, nasty or selfish.
I'm really glad of that,
But in a few minutes, God,
I'm going to get out of bed.
From now on, I'm probably going to need a lot of help.

source unknown

I started this book with my mother's last words. I will also end this book with a reminder of those words—"Live like it's real . . . because it is!" Every day I remember those words. They challenge me. They cause me to live differently. They help me move past my feelings and push through each day connected to my Maker.

On our journey we have explored how to live differently by getting real with God and acknowledging our need to come to him. As we found our way back to the place of a first love relationship with God, we then examined the four core truths of his love for us, as expressed in Psalm 139 by King David.

Following David's expression of eloquent and heartwarming truth about God's involvement in our lives, we took a look at Love's Response. This helped us recognize that the appropriate response would be to reciprocate his love by taking a stand to surrender our lives to him. And now as we read the last part of Psalm 139 we find a path for daily usefulness by staying connected to Christ each day. I call this part "Love's Confession." Take a look with me.

Search me, O God, and know my heart;
    test me and know my anxious thoughts.

198

See if there is any offensive way in me,
and lead me in the way everlasting.

Psalm 139:23–24

Let's wrap up Psalm 139 looking for application for our daily lives:

Core Truths: Start with a New Belief System

Embracing the core truths is the beginning of a change in our perspective and belief system. We have a need to personalize the love of God—bringing it into our own hearts and worlds.

- He knows me.
- He protects me.
- He made me.
- He values me.

Love's Response: Move to the Place of Surrender

We were created to live in relationship with God. Relationships are not one-sided, but they are reciprocal. This is our response to the core truths of God's love and involvement in our lives.

- I choose to take his side.
- I want to love what he loves.
- I want to hate what he hates.
- I choose to live differently.

Love's Confession: Start Each Day with Connection

Daily surrender and confession are the keys to remaining clean and clear before the Lord. In this place, I can be filled with the fresh outpouring of his Holy Spirit. And with that power I can experience being used in the most practical ways for his everyday service.

- Search me.
- Cleanse me.
- Fill me.
- Use me.

As I sat with Psalm 139 during that difficult year in my life, I began to see a clear-cut path. Each day I could be reset to live— really live—in him.

Search Me

Every day is a new opportunity to walk in relationship with God. Time is precious, and the days count. Knowing that this is true, I want to start each new day with the Lord. To do this I begin my day by asking God to search my heart for anything that is displeasing to him or anything that might keep me separated from relationship with him. We often don't realize that we have lived in ways displeasing to God. The big sins are obvious and known, but it's the attitudes of the heart and the imaginations of the mind that we are often in denial about.

Cleanse Me

I have made it a practice to ask the Lord to cleanse me by the blood of Jesus, to be new and fresh each day. This starts my day by acknowledging my humanness before God. I confess my inability to cleanse myself and ask that he would cleanse me and make me a whole, cleansed, pure vessel for his work that day. This is a miracle, because we could not accomplish this in and of ourselves. Left to ourselves we would just carry around our sins day to day like old dirty laundry.

Fill Me

This is the part that gets me excited! By the miracle of his grace, God fills us each day with his presence and power that we might walk in the plans he has prepared for us in his bigger picture of our lives. Without being filled with his Spirit I am left to just live in the flesh—stuck in the crazy cycle of all my old stuff.

Use Me

Most people want to know that their individual life has purpose. The good news is, in Christ each of us can be assured that he has a plan for our lives. Many weekends of the year I am at retreats, sharing the information in this book with women of all ages. It is a privilege for me to repeat the truths that are written within these pages—over and over. I continue to grow as I am refreshed and reminded of the truth. I begin each retreat telling the women that over the next few days we will spend time looking at what it means to live as God's woman. I use an acrostic of the word *woman* to guide our time through the weekend:

W—Wonderful worth
O—Ordained for God's purposes
M—Managing life by faith
A—Attitude of thanks and praise
N—Nearer to God each day

The first two letters outline a message of truth that lays a basic foundation for us as women. When we realize that we have been assigned worth by God and that he does indeed have a purpose for us, we have a solid starting place for everything else. This foundation is not about us—it's all about him. When we embrace the truth, we can get over ourselves and learn how to live for him.

The remainder of the letters are about learning to live in him and for him. With our foundational truths in place we can dare to trust him and manage our lives by faith. As we grow in a relationship of trust and intimacy, we realize that the power for our daily walk is in praising him through all of life's ups and downs. Finally we bring it down to the basic essentials of living—and it's one day at a time growing nearer to God.

- I must acknowledge I am a sinner.
- I must affirm the truth that I have been created "By Him and For Him."
- I must be connected to my Maker.
- I must admit that apart from him I can do nothing of eternal value.
- I must seek to be cleansed so I can live for him.
- I must ask to be filled up with fresh fuel each day for living in him.
- I must be reset by truth.
- I must live in the Spirit and not in my own flesh.
- I must depend on his strength, direction, and leading.

In order for all of this to happen I must be connected. Let's look at the words of Christ in John 15 and see what Christ himself says about our connection.

Remain in me, and I will remain in you. No branch can bear fruit by itself; it must remain in the vine. Neither can you bear fruit unless you remain in me. I am the vine; you are the branches. If a man remains in me and I in him, he will bear much fruit; apart from me you can do nothing. . . . As the Father has loved me, so have I loved you. Now remain in my love. If you obey my commands, you will remain in my love, just as I have obeyed my Father's commands and remain in his love. I have told you this so that my joy may be in you and that your joy may be complete. My command is this: Love each other as I have loved you.

vv. 4–5, 9–12

Later in the chapter he says:

You did not choose me, but I chose you and appointed you to go and bear fruit—fruit that will last.

v. 16

In a nutshell, I have been created by God and for God's purposes. His purpose is that I would love him and love others. (When asked what the greatest commandment was, Jesus himself said it boiled down to two things: "Love the Lord your God with all your heart, soul, and strength. And love your neighbor.") I can only carry out these purposes of God if I am connected to him. When I am connected to him I have the joy of Jesus within me. And that, my friend, is where life gets exciting!

Let's Talk Connection

As I type I am looking at a blow dryer that I have sitting here at my desk. The manufacturer created this blow dryer with a specific purpose in mind—to blow hot air on wet hair to make it dry. (I know, I'm a genius . . . hang in here with me.)

The manufacturer put the blow dryer together with every part it needed to accomplish its purpose. There is only one thing that has to be done before each use . . . drum roll . . . it has to be plugged in to a power source! Without the power it cannot complete its purpose.

Can you imagine how ridiculous it would look if I was standing in front of my mirror with wet hair, moving an unplugged blow dryer around my head. My husband would think I had lost it! But that is how it is with us in our spiritual lives. We run around in circles, trying to make a life of substance with no power connection.

Our manufacturer—Almighty God—created us for a specific purpose: to love him, to love others, and to bear fruit. When we became his we were then equipped with everything we would need to accomplish his designated purpose for us. And just like the blow dryer, only one thing must be done in order to carry out the Maker's plan—we must plug in.

How do we plug in?

Each morning we have a choice. We can seek God or forget about him. Seeking him might look something like the following. Develop a habit of seeking God first thing each morning. Begin your dialogue with him upon rising and continue that dialogue throughout the day. Make it a habit to read Scripture to start your day. This is devotional reading; deeper study can be done at another time. Opening your day with truth takes only a small amount of time, sets the tone for the day, and gives you a spiritual theme to be thinking about as you go about the business of living. Follow the example of King David and ask God to search your heart, cleanse you, fill you, and use you each and every day.

Carry a Scripture with you throughout the day and review it several times—praying it back to God.

An example of a Scripture might be:

> So do not worry, saying, "What shall we eat?" or "What shall we drink?" or "What shall we wear?" For the pagans run after all these things, and your heavenly Father knows that you need them.
>
> Matthew 6:31–32

Look for the key words of truth and determine how to apply it to your own life.

- **Truth:** My heavenly Father knows what I need.
- **Application:** I don't need to worry about things.
- **Prayer:** Father, I thank you that you know what I need. And you will provide what I need. Help me to break the habit of worrying over things. Forgive me for the many times I worry. I thank you that I don't have to worry but can trust you instead.

The Everyday Vessel

I used to think that being "used of God" was about doing things in traditional church ministry. With that as my definition, the ways God could use me were limited.

I was raised to be a singer, so singing in the church and for the Lord became my primary way of being used of God—or so I thought. I was very open to being used in that way if I had time to prepare and advance notice. Trouble is, with that type of ministry, I was used just occasionally or for special occasions. As I got a bit older I moved into teaching women's Bible studies. This was thrilling for me because I loved the Word of God. But even in a weekly format, being used of God was limited to one morning a week for a specified group of church women.

Then it happened. God changed my mind about my definition of being used of God—and it happened in a way I never would have expected. One morning as I was emptying the dishwasher I put away our old worn Tupperware pitcher, placing it on the top shelf of the kitchen cupboard. This is something I did every day. But this particular morning, as I put the Tupperware away, I noticed the beautiful little teapot sitting up high on the same shelf. I took the teapot down, blew the dust off the top, and admired it for a moment. It was shiny, beautifully shaped, and adorned with painted flowers.

Then I began having a little mental dialogue with the pretty little pot.

"Oh, you're such a pretty little teapot. I forgot all about you. It's too bad I can't use you, but if I took you down off the shelf, you'd be broken in no time at all . . . you're much too fragile. Well, I'll just have to save you for special occasions."

And with that last thought I placed the teapot back in its place on the shelf next to the old Tupperware pitcher. Then the "aha" moment came! As I looked at the contrast of the pretty teapot and the Tupperware pitcher, I heard the words *everyday vessel* come from somewhere deep within me. Everyday vessel? I stood staring at my open cupboard for a minute or two, and I got the message loud and clear.

The Tupperware pitcher was useful and practical for everyday use. I could count on it. It wasn't fragile but was strong and reliable. It wasn't pretty, but its look did not affect how useful it was to me. There was no dust gathering on the pitcher because it was being used and washed daily. While the pretty pot sat on the shelf waiting for a special occasion, the pitcher was only perched upon the shelf for short spurts between daily uses.

Clearly I was getting a message—God wanted to make me his everyday vessel. It became clear to me that morning that he desired to use me in the most practical and ordinary of ways. No more waiting for a song to sing or a message to give. He wanted me to be available each and every morning for his service. That service could be as simplistic as being a blessing to someone, cleaning my house, making a meal, or calling a friend. All of life was in his service and had meaning.

Suddenly life was taking on a new and exciting direction. No more wasting my life waiting for opportunity. Now I realized that each and every day is a fresh opportunity to leave "heartprints"— the heartprints of God.

Making Mama Pretty

My mother was in the hospital many times the last year of her life. One particular visit extended to over a week, and her hair was getting out of control. We would tease her and tell her she looked just like Einstein (think—white permed hair gone wild!). She would get a kick out of that, and we would all laugh.

That is, until the evening the doctor came in to tell her she was in need of a delicate surgery the next morning. She signed on the dotted line, and the doctor left. As soon as he was out of earshot, she said, "I can't go down to surgery looking like this! Those young doctors will think I am just a crazy old woman and won't try to save me. I need to have something done to my hair!"

Shocked, I said, "Mom, they don't care what you look like."

"But I do!" she snapped back.

"Okay, I know some hairdressers from church. I'll call one of them and have her come do your hair early tomorrow morning."

"No! They'll think I'm crazy to worry about my hair at a time like this."

I took a breath. "Well, what do you want me to do?"

"I want you to do it."

To that I said "Fine!" and she said "Fine!" and I kissed her and told her I would be there bright and early.

What was I thinking? I have trouble doing my own hair, and hers was clearly going to be a challenge. I went home that night and got out a pretty gift bag and filled it with my supplies—curling iron, brush, lipstick, mirror, and the scissors that I used to cut the kids' bangs—just in case.

The next morning I grabbed my cheery little bag and headed for the hospital. Entering her room just before daylight I found her sitting up in bed, waiting for me. She took one look in my direction and said, "Short. I want it very short."

My mind raced. *Short? She's got to be kidding.* Suddenly I remembered I brought the scissors that I used to trim bangs. *Oh no . . . Lord, I have no idea how to really cut hair.*

"Mom, do you mind if I say a prayer?" So I prayed, "Jesus, I'm asking you to be the hairdresser today. My mom wants her hair short, and I'm asking you to make my mama pretty before she goes into surgery. And I ask this in Jesus's name, amen."

The elderly woman in the next bed chimed in with an amen. "I'm praying with you, honey!" she said.

Whew! It's a good thing because I need all the help I can get.

I began cutting away at Mom's Einstein locks and singing her favorite old chorus. Before I knew it, my new prayer partner joined in, and together we belted out each note of the song.

By now puffs of white hair were all over my mom. I cleaned her up and got the curling iron out. As I finished up I was shocked at how short it was and how pretty she looked. I showed her the mirror, and she smiled. "Looking good!"

About this time the nurse came in to get her ready to go downstairs. She looked at my mother, picked up her wrist, and looked at the name on the wristband. She peered over her glasses and looked at the name on her clipboard. Finally, seeming confused, she said, "Irene?"

"That's me," my mom said with a smile.

"Well, Irene, you look like you've been to the beauty shop."

At this, the lady in the next bed said, "God's beauty shop, honey, God's beauty shop."

The nurse looked at me and said, "I didn't know you did hair."

"Oh, I don't."

"But God does, honey, God does," said the woman from the next bed.

After the nurse finished her details she must have gone out to tell the other nurses, because one by one they filtered through the room, wishing my mother well and smiling at me. They all knew the seriousness of the surgery to be done that morning and were clearly touched by what just took place in that room.

I walked beside the gurney as they took my mom to the surgical floor. And when I could go no further toward the double doors my mom leaned back, looked over her shoulder, raised her arm up, and said, "Thank you for making your mama pretty."

As fast as my legs would take me I made my way into my minivan in the parking lot. I began to cry—partly because I was afraid for my mom and partly because I was in awe of God. I sat there thinking, *This is what it means to be an everyday vessel.* God wants to use us in the most unexpected ways, empowering us to do the things we cannot do, to bring a blessing and hope to another person. I pulled myself together and met my sister in the waiting room. Mom never had the surgery that day. They brought her out because she wasn't stable enough for them to proceed. She died several months later.

Being an everyday vessel is part of the grand purpose of God. He uses ordinary people, clay pot people, to be his hands, his mouth, and his touch. Wherever we go we have the opportunity of leaving heartprints of compassion, understanding, and love. The same way we leave our fingerprints on everything our hands touch, we can now leave heartprints as God sends us out into our ordinary world to be his instruments.

Along the way, if someone should sense his touch through our lives, may we always remember that it is God and his love touching others through ordinary, everyday vessels. What a wonderful way to view each day—Lord, send me out to leave heartprints!

Having the Time of Your Life!

You know, life with Jesus can be like an "E ticket" ride. When I was a child, Disneyland had ticket books. The A ticket was for the boring rides—like Abraham Lincoln Theater. The E ticket was for the best ride in the park—which back then was the Matterhorn. In our lives with the Lord, we get to choose. Will we live with the A ticket or the E ticket? I want the E ticket! I want everything that God has planned for me. What about you? Which life do you want?

I have grieved over the loss of dreams. I have worried that I was in God's Plan B and had missed Plan A because of wrong decisions. I have lived as if everything was all up to me. And now I know that God truly is the one who conforms things according to his plan, prepares us for that plan, and desires to use us to fulfill that plan.

The Bible wasn't the only thing I couldn't look at when I was in so much pain many years ago—I also could not sing a note. My ex-husband and I used to do music together, and when he left the music was gone. Every time I tried to sing I would just cry. This was a huge loss, because music had been a part of my life since I was a small child. Over time as I healed, the music came back. I found myself singing a lot—in the shower, in the car, on the elevator; everywhere I went there was a new song in my heart. Though I never sang in front of others, the music was back, and the ability to worship and praise flooded me with joy.

Ray kept telling me that I should sing publicly again and use the gift God had given me. I explained to him how I had my chance when I was younger but had laid it all down a long time ago. Still he persisted that I should use the gift of music.

"You just don't understand, Ray. You don't start doing music in your fifties!"

And then out of the blue I was offered a recording contract at age fifty-one! Now, go figure—like Sarah having a baby at one hundred! But I get what God is doing—he is going to use the voice he gave me as another everyday vessel. Remember David in the pit? Well, that verse ends with, "He put a new song in my mouth. . . . Many will see and fear and put their trust in the LORD" (Ps. 40:3).

I don't want to be known as an author, a speaker, a director of women's ministries, or a singer—I don't even want to be known just as a mother, friend, or wife. No, I want to be known as a follower of Christ, a woman simply belonging to him. And in this identity, in this position, I can live with passion and freedom unlike anything I have ever known. In this place it's no longer about me. It's about a bigger, grander picture, and a big loving God who created us with a purpose!

God Does Great Things in Our Lives

Being a woman, I always like to know where the story is going or how the story ends. When I go to a movie, I can't stand it when the story trails off into the sunset—I want to know at least a little of what happened out in that sunset. So, though my story doesn't end here, I will give you a glimpse out into our sunset.

Our family has grown up. Beginning with four children who were in kindergarten, first grade, and third grade, we now have children who are twenty-three, twenty-five, and twenty-seven. Ray and I are most grateful for God plopping us into each other's lives. Our lives aren't perfect, and we work through the same things that all couples do—we have our stuff! But even in the stuff, we thank God for the puzzle pieces that don't make sense but end up being part of the bigger picture. I could not have asked for a more loving husband. He has stood beside me, being patient while I wrestled, grew, and healed. Ray is definitely one of the above-and-beyond-anything-I-could-hope-for pieces in my life. Together we now have the privilege of supporting blended families with the same hope, challenge, and comfort God has given us.

As I wrap up this last chapter I am admittedly a bit emotional. Writing a book, and especially one so personal, is a bit like having a baby. There are labor pains along the way, and finally the day comes when you hit one last stroke on the keyboard. You hope that you said everything you wanted to say, made some sense, and that what you said can be used to make a difference in someone's life.

I know God can do great things in your life and mine. I know that he not only can but wants to. I also know that as you embrace the truth of who you are, your life will change.

With that change will come a new passion to live out your purpose as his.

Oh . . . it's so exciting to be living as his that I just want to shout right now! But it's about one o'clock in the morning, and I'll wake up the entire house if I do. Oh yes, just one last thing: remember, I promised my mother to always remind the women to "live like it's real, because it is!"

So I will end with this:

Live like Christ is real, true, and worth trusting.

Live like who you are in Christ is real.

Live like his Spirit living inside you is real.

Live like everything that has been promised is real.

Live like heaven is real.

I still hear him calling, "Come to me."

Can you hear him too?

For Further Reflection

1. Read Psalm 139:23–24. This is Love's Confession.
2. Do you ask God to search you daily? Are you aware that we don't even know that sometimes our hearts need to be cleansed?
3. How can understanding that God fills us with his power and his Spirit change our view of personal purpose in daily living?
4. What does the concept of an everyday vessel mean to you?
5. Can you live like the presence and purpose of God is real in your life? What would that change? How would you change?

Notes

Introduction

1. Oswald Chambers, *My Utmost for His Highest* (Grand Rapids: Discovery House, 1992), December 3 reading.

Chapter 2 Believing I'm Not Enough

1. Henri Nouwen, *Life of the Beloved* (New York: Crossroad, 1992), 21.
2. Susan Young, "Trends," *ANG Newspaper, Inside Bay Area*, February 27, 2001.

Chapter 3 No More Hiding

1. Simon Tugwell, *The Beatitudes* (Springfield, IL: Templegate, 1990), 130.
2. A.W. Tozer, *Gems from Tozer* (Camp Hill, PA: Christian Publishers, 1969), 8.
3. Chambers, *My Utmost for His Highest*, June 11 reading.

Chapter 4 His

1. Brennan Manning, *Abba's Child* (Colorado Springs: NavPress, 1994), 55.
2. Chambers, *My Utmost for His Highest*, September 4 reading.
3. Robert S. McGee, *The Search for Significance* (Houston: Rapha, 1985), 14.

Chapter 5 Transformed by Truth

1. Chambers, *My Utmost for His Highest*, January 1 reading.
2. Manning, *Abba's Child*, 19.

Chapter 7 God Protects Me

1. Bob Coy, *Dreamality* (West Monroe, LA: Howard Publishing, 2005), 83.
2. Ibid., 143.

Chapter 9 God Values Me

1. McGee, *The Search for Significance*, 14.
2. *Vine's Expository Dictionary of Biblical Words* (Nashville: Thomas Nelson), 1985.
3. William Backus and Marie Chapian, *Telling Yourself the Truth* (Minneapolis: Bethany House, 1980), 27.
4. Ibid., 29.
5. McGee, *The Search for Significance*, 27.
6. Backus and Chapian, *Telling Yourself the Truth*, 41.
7. Ibid., 35.

Chapter 10 Choosing a New Direction

1. Max Lucado, *Just Like Jesus* (Nashville: Word, 1998), 3–4.

Chapter 11 Choosing a Life of Dependence

1. Lucado, *Just Like Jesus*, 4.

Debbie Alsdorf is a popular speaker and author and the director of women's ministries at Cornerstone Fellowship in Livermore, California. Debbie's weekly Bible studies are attended by hundreds of women who are eager to discover how to deepen their walk with God. In addition, as the founder of Design4Living Ministries, Debbie also leads conferences and retreats that equip and encourage women in their faith. She and her husband, Ray, have raised a blended family of four adult children, and they currently live with two dogs and one cat. To have Debbie speak at your event or to host a Design4Living day at your church, contact Debbie at www.design4living.org.